Critical acclaim for t[...]

"[The Berkeley Guides are] brimming with useful information for the low-budget traveler—material delivered in a fresh, funny, and often irreverent way." —*The Philadelphia Inquirer*

"The [Berkeley Guides] are deservedly popular because of their extensive coverage, entertaining style of writing, and heavy emphasis on budget travel...If you are looking for tips on hostels, vegetarian food, and hitchhiking, there are no books finer." —*San Diego Union-Tribune*

"Straight dirt on everything from hostels to look for and beaches to avoid to museums least likely to attract your parents... they're fresher than Harvard's Let's Go series." —*Seventeen*

"The [Berkeley Guides] give a rare glimpse into the real cultures of Europe, Canada, Mexico, and the United States...with in-depth historical backgrounds on each place and a creative, often poetical style of prose." —*Eugene Weekly*

"More comprehensive, informative and witty than Let's Go." —*Glamour*

"The Berkeley Guides have more and better maps, and on average, the nuts and bolts descriptions of such things as hotels and restaurants tend to be more illuminating than the often terse and sometimes vague entries in the Let's Go guides." —*San Jose Mercury News*

"These well-organized guides list can't-miss sights, offbeat attractions and cheap thrills, such as festivals and walks. And they're fun to read." —*New York Newsday*

"Written for the young and young at heart...you'll find this thick, fact-filled guide makes entertaining reading." —*St. Louis Dispatch*

"Bright articulate guidebooks. The irreverent yet straight-forward prose is easy to read and offers a sense of the adventures awaiting travelers off the beaten path." —*Portland Oregonian*

BERKELEY

budget
guides

On the Loose
On the Cheap
Off the Beaten Path

THE BERKELEY GUIDES

California '97
Central America (2nd Edition)
Eastern Europe (3rd Edition)
Europe '97
France (4th Edition)
Germany & Austria (4th Edition)
Great Britain & Ireland '97
Italy '97
London '97
Mexico '97
New York City '97
Pacific Northwest & Alaska (3rd Edition)
Paris (3rd Edition)
San Francisco '97

Fodor's **BERKELEY** budget guides

france

fourth edition

On the Loose
On the Cheap
Off the Beaten Path

WRITTEN BY BERKELEY STUDENTS IN COOPERATION WITH
THE ASSOCIATED STUDENTS OF THE UNIVERSITY OF CALIFORNIA

ISBN 0–679–03177–4

Fourth Edition

THE BERKELEY GUIDE TO FRANCE

Editors: Sarah Fallon, Mielikki Org
Managing Editors: Tara Duggan, Kristina Malsberger, Sora Song
Executive Editor: Sharron Wood
Creative Director: Fabrizio La Rocca
Cartographers: David Lindroth, Inc.; Eureka Cartography
Text Design: Tigist Getachew
Cover Art: Poul Lange (3-D art), Catherine Karnow/WoodFin Camp (photo in frame), Paul D'Innocenzo (still life and digital imaging)
Cover Design: Fabrizio La Rocca

SPECIAL SALES

The Berkeley Guides and all Fodor's Travel Publications are available at special discounts for bulk purchases for sales promotions or premiums. Special editions, including personalized covers, excerpts of existing guides, and corporate imprints, can be created in large quantities for special needs. For more information, contact your local bookseller or write to Special Markets, Fodor's Travel Publications, 201 E. 50th Street, New York, NY 10022. Inquiries from Canada should be directed to your local Canadian bookseller or sent to Random House of Canada, Ltd., Marketing Department, 1265 Aerowood Drive, Mississauga, Ontario L4W 1B9. Inquiries from the United Kingdom should be sent to Fodor's Travel Publications, 20 Vauxhall Bridge Road, London, England SW1V 2SA.

PRINTED IN THE UNITED STATES OF AMERICA

10 9 8 7 6 5 4 3 2 1

Contents

What to do when your *money* is done traveling before you are.

Don't worry. With **MoneyGram**,℠ your parents can send you money in usually 10 minutes or less to more than 18,000 locations in 86 countries. So if the money you need to see history becomes history, call us and we'll direct you to a **MoneyGram**℠ agent closest to you.

USA: **1-800-MONEYGRAM**
Germany: **0130-8-16629**

Canada: **1-800-933-3278**
England: **0800-89-7198**
or call collect **303-980-3340**

France: **05-905311**
Spain: **900-96-1218**

MoneyGram
MONEY IN MINUTES WORLDWIDE ℠

What the Berkeley Guides Are All About

Four years ago, a motley bunch of U.C. Berkeley students launched a new series of guidebooks—*The Berkeley Guides*. Since then, we've been busy writing and editing 14 books to destinations across the globe, from California, Mexico, and Central America to Europe and Eastern Europe. Along the way our writers have weathered bus plunges, rabies, and guerrilla attacks, landed bush planes above the Arctic Circle, gotten lost in the woods (proverbially and literally), and broken bread with all sorts of peculiar characters—from Mafia dons and Hell's Angel bikers to all those lunatics on the Métro. And don't forget about the train station sleep-ins, voodoo bus schedules, and hotel owners that just don't get it ("you only want *to see* a room? Non, c'est impossible.")

Coordinating the efforts of 65 U.C. Berkeley writers back at the office is an equally daunting task (have you ever tried to track manuscript from Morocco?). But that's the whole point of *The Berkeley Guides*: to bring you the most up-to-date info on prices, the latest budget-travel trends, the newest restaurants and hostels, where to catch your next train—all written and edited by people who know what cheap travel is all about.

You see, it's one of life's weird truisms that the more cheaply you travel, the more you inevitably experience. If you're looking for five-star meals, air-conditioned tour buses, and reviews of the same old tourist traps, you're holding the wrong guidebook. Instead, *The Berkeley Guides* give you an in-depth look at local culture, detailed coverage of small towns and off-beat sights, bars and cafés where tourists rarely tread, plus no-nonsense practical info that deals with the real problems of real people (where to get aspirin at 3 AM, where to launder those dirty socks).

Coming from a community as diverse as Berkeley, we also wanted our guides to be useful to everyone, so we tell you if a place is wheelchair accessible, if it provides resources for gay and lesbian travelers, and if it's safe for women traveling solo. Many of us are Californians, which means most of us like trees and mountain trails. It also means we emphasize the outdoors in every *Berkeley Guide* and include lots of info about hiking and tips on protecting the environment.

Most important, these guides are for travelers who want to see more than just the main sights. We find out what local people do for fun, where they go to eat, drink, or just hang out. Most guidebooks lead you down the tourist trail, ignoring important local issues, events, and culture. In *The Berkeley Guides* we give you the information you need to understand what's going on around you, whether it's the scoop on student protests or the latest shenanigans of French president Jacques Chirac.

We've done our best to make sure the information in *The Berkeley Guides* is accurate, but time doesn't stand still: prices change, places go out of business, currencies get devalued. Call ahead when it's really important, and try not to get too stressed out.

Thanks to You

Some might say that the French aren't a friendly bunch, but don't tell that to our writers, who relied on the hospitality and cooperation of friendly French folk as they bused, biked, and hiked their way through France. From explaining how to operate automatic toilets to giving the lowdown on the bar scene in the Marais (and the Marais Poitevin), natives were glad to lend a cigarette, chat, and point our writers the right direction. We'd like to thank the following people—as well as the hundreds of others whom our writers encountered along the way—for the encouragement, stories, and free drinks:

The Baillets (Paris); Franck Barthe (Paris); François Bel (Paris); Adam Bloom (for the tomatoes and ride to Annecy); Jean-Yves Boisson (Paris); Jannick Bourles (Paris); Pierre and Sylvaine Briand (Paris); Paul Burgin (San Diego, CA); Emily Buttinger (Seattle, WA); Chantal and Fabrice (Bourg-St-Maurice); Alain Charon (Paris); François Charon (Paris); the Chouvets (Aux Cadrans, Paris); Jean-Pierre et Françoise Clauzel (Pyla-sur-Mer); Marlene Colburn (New York, NY); Harry Cover (Pierre's Produce); Alison Desposito (San Francisco, CA); Mme Devigne (Paris); Adam Diamant (Berkeley, CA); Mary Pat Dorr and the Catalina crew; François Dumarais (Morvan); the Fallons (Washington, D.C.); Pierre Gaconnet (Paris); Mom and Dad Gierlich (Los Angeles, CA); Nils Gilman (Paris); Anne-Marie Godfrey (Encinitas, CA); Elisabeth Höchtl (Austria); Joanna Honikman (Berkeley, CA); the Houyels (Aix-en-Provence); Isabelle and Olivier (Paris); Jacques (Bergerac); Olivier Joly (Paris and Lyon); Julia and friends (Paris); Julien, the killer sandwich maker (Chamonix); Noemi Kubiak (Paris); Andrew Lakoff (Paris); Large Pachyderm (Los Angeles, CA); Odile and Jean-Luc Legoff (Lannilis); Sophie Macé (Paris); Mamette (Ploumanach); Marie-Thérèse Le Mindu (Ploumanach); Sister Monica (Lyon); Fiona Morrisson (Bordeaux); Morten and Geir (Norway); Gerard Mulot (Paris); Jacqueline Noverra (Nancy); Maman et Papa Org (Encinitas, CA); Pascale and Philippe (Toulouse); Dominique Prévot (Morvan); Fabrice Raymond (Paris); François Régis (Morvan); Françoise and Xavier Renoux (La Rochelle); Marine Renoux (La Rochelle); Robert Reungoat (Le Conquet); Melissa de la Rosa (Oakland, CA); Mylah de la Rosa (Oakland, CA); Dominique and Yves Schneider-Maunoury (Aix-en-Provence); Annick Sher (Brest); Jeremy Sokulsky (Boston, MA); Jacques Strappe (Pierre's Pleasuredome); Pavel and Joy Švihra (CA); the Sweeneys (Los Angeles, CA); Kathryn Tuma (Paris); the Vasseurs (Nojaret, Lyon, and Paris); Marsu Villani (Paris); San Vu Ngoc (Grenoble); the Vu Ngoc Family (Palaiseau); Marjilein Westerbeek (Paris); Amy Zsigo (Berkeley, CA).

Back in Berkeley, Maureen Klier and especially Kathleen Dodge provided invaluable help in both the early and final stages of this book, and Suzanne Stein kept us all from losing our heads. We'd also like to thank the Random House folks who helped us with cartography, page design, and production: Bob Blake, Ellen Browne, Denise DeGennaro, Tigist Getachew, Laura Kidder, Fabrizio La Rocca, and Linda Schmidt.

Berkeley Bios

Behind every restaurant blurb, write-up, lodging review, and introduction in this book lurks a U.C. Berkeley writer. Maybe you know the type—perpetually short on time, money, and clean clothes. Six Berkeley students spent the summer in France researching and writing this book; every two weeks they sent their manuscript back to Berkeley, where Millie and Sarah whipped, squashed, and pummeled it into shape.

The Writers

French native **Emmanuel Briand** and his pet computer Max, which doubled as a pillow, traveled light to stay one step ahead of both the French police (they were trying to throw his butt into boot camp so he could complete his military service) and his stomach (he's still suffering indigestion from adjectives). The laws of France and grammar aside, he managed to give five chapters of *The Berkeley Guide to France* a facelift. After burning through six pairs of espadrilles and a few hundred Hamlet cigarillos, Emmanuel is convinced that there are way too many old cathedrals in France, and he's developed a strange fascination for industrial port towns. You might still find him in a fisherman's pub in Brittany, in front of *une petite mousse*, boasting of how he killed wild boars with his ancestor Obélix in the Morvan, drank cognac with Jean Louis Lebris (a.k.a. Jack) de Kerouac in Brest, and wasted time with Marcel Proust in the shadow of the young blossoming girls of Cabourg.

The Berkeley Guides plucked **Shane Christensen** from the depths of the Amazon, where he had been swinging aimlessly from tree to tree, and sent him halfway around the world with a serious purpose: to unearth the sensual pleasures of southern France on a *très petit* budget. Shane's dream of conquering the assignment from the back of a Harley was crushed by financial realities, although he did look pretty cool cruising the Corniches on a 50cc scooter. When he wasn't at a beachside café, sipping *pastis* and pretending his manuscripts were a Hemingway story in the making, he was on the beach, happily dodging the onslaught of postgraduate angst (not to mention unemployment) that follows a summer tour in France.

Once again, **Marisa Gierlich** (actually Gierlich-Burgin, now) went traipsing off to Europe when she probably should have been at home on the beach. But after writing for five Berkeley Guides titles and two Lonely Planet titles, it's become sort of a habit. Marisa graduated from U.C. Berkeley with an English degree in 1992 and ever since, she's been dispelling the myth that travel writing is a glamorous job.

After attending to the Mexican side of her genes by writing for the *Berkeley Guide to Mexico 1996*, **Viviana Mahieux** decided to ignore her French heritage no longer (not that her unpronounceable last name lets her forget it). Her stay in Paris left her hopelessly addicted to coffee and taught her ways to avoid the question: "What can you do with a degree in comparative literature and history?" She is now wavering between a lifelong career in denial or going to grad school to get a highly utilitarian PhD in literature.

Although she still thinks Prague is the best city on earth, **Julia Švihra** found Paris not a bad little town. Taste-testing *chocolat à l'ancienne* at salons throughout the city and, er, revising the Berkeley Guide, it was her unrelenting quest for France's culinary delights that sustained her through bike rides in torrential rains and mysterious allergies. Her quest also took her to the dim nooks and crannies of villages in the Ile-de-France and Champagne. Special thanks must go to Andrew Lakoff, extraordinary traveling companion, and Gérard Mulot, extraordinary baker.

Leaving her fate in the hands of French drivers and letting adventure have its way, **Michelle Sweeney** set off through southwest France on her bicycle. Her escapades began just after touchdown in the Charles de Gaulle airport: She lugged 70 kilograms of bike and luggage through the underground halls of the Paris Métro and past gaping onlookers in front of the Paris Opéra. From the crowded streets in Paris to solitary mountain passes, helpful hands, shouts, and signs of encouragement accompanied her every step of the way. Not least among those who helped out were Jeremy Sokulsky, her sometimes riding companion who kept her going through lonely hours of writing, and the Clauzel family, who offered her refuge from a suspicious pursuant, shared stories over a bowl of ice cream, and christened her bike Monsieur Cyclopède. To find out about breakneck descents, romantic sunsets, hedgehog tentmates, expatriate surf colonies, and the adventures that transpired in the 900 ensuing kilometers, keep an eye out for *The Adventures of Monsieur Cyclopède,* on café shelves and free paper kiosks near you.

The Editors

Sarah Fallon once got booted out of France ("deported" is the word actually scrawled in her passport) for not having a visa. Impervious to her pleas, French officials sent her back to Baden-Baden (the horror), where she spent a creepy night in an abandoned movie theater. She went on to violate other aspects of the French legal code, though she thinks it prudent not to mention them here. She is now living less dangerously in Berkeley.

After defending herself from pyromaniacal strikers and uttering enough expletives to make even a French person take notice, **Mielikki Org** managed a hasty exit from Orly airport and hustled herself back to Berkeley in time to edit the books she wrote for in 1996—*The Berkeley Guide to Paris* and *The Berkeley Guide to France.* In an effort to cope with bouts of pen-envy ("I wrote that line—don't change it!") and travel withdrawal, Millie tried holding her writers' plane tickets for ransom. Thankfully, someone was able to cough up a bottle of Sauternes and wrench the soggy tickets from her teeth. After trudging through thousands of pages of manuscript, Millie and Sarah know two things for sure: that they're going to have the vacation of their lives if they ever make it back to France, and that those floor chains and desk handcuffs can get darn uncomfortable.

France

ENGLAND

La Manche
(English Channel)

Cala
Boulogne

Cherbourg
Fécamp
Dieppe
An
Etretat
Le Havre
Honfleur
Royen
Coutances
Bayeux
Caen
Seine
Ile de
Bréhat
Granville
NORMANDY
Giverny
Ile
d'Ouessant
Perros-Guirec
Roscoff
St-Malo
Avranches
Versailles
Brest
Morlaix
Dinan
Fougères
St-Brieuc
Chartres
Quimper
BRITTANY
Quimperlé
Rennes
Concarneau
Vannes
Vitré
Le Mans
Lorient
Chan
Quiberon
Angers
Blois
Belle-Ile
Saumur
Loire
Tours
Nantes
PAYS DE
LA LOIRE

ATLANTIC
OCEAN

Les Sables-
d'Olonne
Poitiers
LO
VA
Niort
Ile de Ré
La Rochelle
POITOU
CHARENTES
Cognac
Limoges
Angoulême
LIMOUSI

Bay of Biscay
Périgueux
Brive-la-
Gaillarde
Bordeaux
Garonne
Sarlat
Dordogne
Rocamado
Cahors
AQUITAINE
Montauban
Alb
Bayonne
MIDI-
PYRENEES
Toulouse
Biarritz
Pau
St-Jean-Pied-
de-Port
Carcassonne

N

Rail Lines

0   50 mi

0   75 km

S P A I N

ANDORRA

France

BELGIUM

THE NORTH

Lille

Arras

LUXEMBOURG

PICARDY

Beauvais

Reims

Metz

Paris

ILE-DE-FRANCE

Châlons-sur-Marne

Nancy

Saverne

Strasbourg

GERMANY

CHAMPAGNE

Troyes

ALSACE-LORRAINE

Colmar

Auxerre

Mulhouse

Vézelay

Belfort

Dijon

Besançon

Bourges

Beaune

Nevers

BURGUNDY

Dole

Chalon-Sur-Saône

FRANCHE-COMTE

SWITZERLAND

Montluçon

Mâcon

RHONE-ALPS

Clermont-Ferrand

Lyon

Annecy

Chamonix

AUVERGNE

Vienne

Voiron

Chambéry

ITALY

Aurillac

Le Puy

Grenoble

Rhône

Valence

Rodez

Millau

Orange

PROVENCE

RIVIERA

Menton

Nîmes

Avignon

Nice

MONACO

LANGUEDOC
ROUSSILLON

Montpellier

Arles

Aix-en-Provence

Monte Carlo

Antibes

Béziers

Cannes

St-Raphaël

Marseille

St-Tropez

Narbonne

Toulon

Perpignan

Île-Rousse

Mediterranean Sea

Calvi

Bastia

CORSICA

Rhine

Saône

BASICS 1

If you've ever traveled with anyone before, you know the two types of people in the world—the planners and the nonplanners. You also know that travel brings out the very worst in both groups: Left to their own devices, the planners will have you goose-stepping from attraction to attraction on a cultural blitzkrieg, while the nonplanners will invariably miss the flight, the bus, and the point. This Basics chapter offers you a middle ground; we hope it provides enough information to help plan your trip to France without saddling you with an itinerary or invasion plan. Keep in mind that companies go out of business and prices inevitably go up. Remain flexible; if you want predictability, stay home and watch reruns of *Baywatch*.

Planning Your Trip

WHEN TO GO

Like many of her European neighbors, France is swamped with travelers during the summer months, especially after June 29, when all the European schools get out. Unless you care to spend your time with thousands of your closest American (and German, and Italian, and Spanish . . .) friends, avoid travel during July and August, when prices are higher, crowds are bigger, and you may be hard-pressed to find a space in hotels and hostels. To experience more temperate weather and less harried locals, travel during the late spring or early fall. However, summer travel does hold some advantages: more trains and buses, busier nightlife, and tons of festivals.

NATIONAL HOLIDAYS France is a Catholic country and observes many holidays derived from the Church calendar. If a holiday falls on a Tuesday or Thursday, many businesses *font le pont* (make the bridge) and close on that Monday or Friday, too. Here's a list of major holidays:

January 1; Easter Monday; May 1 (Labor Day); **May 8** (World War II Armistice Day—a new holiday not observed as extensively as others); **Ascension** (five weeks after Easter); **Whit Monday** (late May or early June); **July 14** (Bastille Day); **August 15** (Assumption Day); **November 1** (All Saints' Day); **November 11** (World War I Armistice); and **December 25** (Christmas).

FESTIVALS France loves to fête. Most festivals are region- or town-specific and will be covered in the appropriate chapters, but a few of the biggies are mentioned here. Pay attention to when festivals occur in your travels, not only because you're dying to be part of the fun, but because lodging can become especially tight around these times.

February ushers in **Carnival,** celebrated in towns throughout the country, most notably in Nice. Parades and general partying are enjoyed before Lent spoils the fun. May 1 is **May Day,** a cel-

1

ebration honoring workers worldwide. Trade unions organize marches, and street vendors sell lilies of the valley, a symbol of the labor movement. The **Cannes Film Festival** on the French Riviera also happens in late May, as does the **French Open Tennis Championship,** which brings the world's best players to Roland Garros Stadium in Paris. The **Fête de la Musique** explodes on June 21, the summer solstice, bringing live music to streets, cafés, and impromptu outdoor venues all over France. By far the biggest French national holiday is **Bastille Day** on July 14, celebrating the storming of the state prison in 1789 that kicked off the Revolution. The **Tour de France,** the world's most famous bicycle race, wends its way through France in June and July, winding up on the Champs-Elysées on the fourth Sunday in July. In towns all along the route, celebrations precede the Tour's arrival by a week or so. September and October see *vendanges* (grape harvests) begin, and local festivals pop up in towns throughout the wine regions.

GOVERNMENT TOURIST OFFICES

IN THE UNITED STATES The **French Government Tourist Offices** can mail you a stack of shiny brochures that advertise travel packages like "Paris Aristocrat" and "Monte Carlo Magnifique." If you want to ask specific questions, call their Information Center (tel. 900/990–0040) and pay 50¢ per minute (9 AM–7 PM EST). *444 Madison Ave., 16th Floor, New York, NY 10022; 676 N. Michigan Ave., Suite 3360, Chicago, IL 60611; 9454 Wilshire Blvd., Suite 715, Los Angeles, CA 90212.*

IN CANADA Maison de la France. *1981 av. McGill Collège, Suite 490, Montréal, Qué. H3A 2W9, tel. 514/288–4264; 30 St. Patrick St., Suite 700, Toronto, Ont. M5T 3A3, tel. 416/593–4723.*

Council Travel Offices in the United States

ARIZONA: Tempe (tel. 602/966–3544). CALIFORNIA: Berkeley (tel. 510/848–8604), Davis (tel. 916/752–2285), La Jolla (tel. 619/452–0630), Long Beach (tel. 310/598–3338), Los Angeles (tel. 310/208–3551), Palo Alto (tel. 415/325–3888), San Diego (tel. 619/270–6401), San Francisco (tel. 415/421–3473 or 415/566–6222), Santa Barbara (tel. 805/562–8080). COLORADO: Boulder (tel. 303/447–8101), Denver (tel. 303/571–0630). CONNECTICUT: New Haven (tel. 203/562–5335). FLORIDA: Miami (tel. 305/670–9261). GEORGIA: Atlanta (tel. 404/377–9997). ILLINOIS: Chicago (tel. 312/951–0585), Evanston (tel. 847/475–5070). INDIANA: Bloomington (tel. 812/330–1600). IOWA: Ames (tel. 515/296–2326). KANSAS: Lawrence (tel. 913/749–3900). LOUISIANA: New Orleans (tel. 504/866–1767). MARYLAND: College Park (301/779–1172). MASSACHUSETTS: Amherst (tel. 413/256–1261), Boston (tel. 617/266–1926), Cambridge (tel. 617/497–1497 or 617/225–2555). MICHIGAN: Ann Arbor (tel. 313/998–0200). MINNESOTA: Minneapolis (tel. 612/379–2323). NEW YORK: New York (tel. 212/822–2700, 212/666–4177, or 212/254–2525). NORTH CAROLINA: Chapel Hill (tel. 919/942–2334). OHIO: Columbus (tel. 614/294–8696). OREGON: Portland (tel. 503/228–1900). PENNSYLVANIA: Philadelphia (tel. 215/382–0343), Pittsburgh (tel. 412/683–1881). RHODE ISLAND: Providence (tel. 401/331–5810). TENNESSEE: Knoxville (tel. 423/523–9900). TEXAS: Austin (tel. 512/472-4931), Dallas (tel. 214/363–9941). UTAH: Salt Lake City (tel. 801/582–5840). WASHINGTON: Seattle (tel. 206/632–2448 or 206/329–4567). WASHINGTON, D.C. (tel. 202/337–6464). For U.S. cities not listed, call tel. 800/2–COUNCIL.

IN THE UNITED KINGDOM French Government Tourist Office. *178 Piccadilly, London W1V OAL, tel. 0171/629-1272.*

DOWN UNDER French Tourist Office. *BNP Building, 12th Floor, 12 Castlereagh St., Sydney, N.S.W. 2000, tel. 02/231-5244.*

BUDGET TRAVEL ORGANIZATIONS

The **Council on International Educational Exchange** ("Council" for short) is a private, nonprofit organization that administers work, volunteer, academic, and professional programs worldwide. Its travel division, **Council Travel**, is a full-service travel agency specializing in student, youth, and budget travel. They offer discounted airfares, rail passes, accommodations, guidebooks, budget tours, and travel gear. They also issue the ISIC, GO25, and ITIC identity cards (*see* Student ID Cards, *below*), as well as Hostelling International cards. Forty-six Council Travel offices serve the budget traveler in the United States, and there are about a dozen overseas, including **Paris** (22 rue des Pyramides, 1er, tel. 01-44-55-55-65) and **Nice** (37 bis rue d'Angleterre, tel. 04-93-82-23-33). Council also puts out a variety of publications, including the free *Student Travels* magazine, a gold mine of travel tips (including info on work- and study-abroad opportunities). *205 E. 42nd St., New York, NY 10017, tel. toll-free 888/COUNCIL, http://www.ciee.org.*

Educational Travel Center (ETC) books low-cost flights to destinations within the continental United States and around the world. Their best deals are on flights leaving the Midwest, especially Chicago. ETC also issues Hostelling International cards. For more details request their free brochure, *Taking Off. 438 N. Frances St., Madison, WI 53703, tel. 608/256-5551.*

STA Travel, the world's largest travel organization catering to students and young people, has over 100 offices worldwide and offers low-price airfares to destinations around the globe, as well as rail passes, car rentals, tours, you name it. STA issues the ISIC and the GO25 youth cards (*see* Student ID Cards, *below*), both of which prove eligibility for student airfares and other travel discounts. Their useful web site is at http://www.sta-travel.com. Call 800/777-0112 or the nearest STA office (*see box, below*) for more info.

Student Flights, Inc. specializes in student and faculty airfares and sells rail passes, ISE cards (*see* Student ID Cards, *below*), and travel guidebooks. *5010 E. Shea Blvd. Suite A104, Scottsdale, AZ 85254, tel. 602/951-1177 or 800/255-8000.*

STA Offices

- **UNITED STATES. CALIFORNIA:** Berkeley (tel. 510/642-3000), Los Angeles (tel. 213/934-8722), San Francisco (tel. 415/391-8407). **MASSACHUSETTS:** Boston (tel. 617/266-6014), Cambridge (tel. 617/576-4623). **NEW YORK:** Columbia University (tel. 212/865-2700), West Village (tel. 212/627-3111). **PENNSYLVANIA:** Philadelphia (tel. 215/382-2928). **WASHINGTON:** Seattle (tel. 206/633-5000). **WASHINGTON, D.C.** (tel. 202/887-0912).

- **INTERNATIONAL. AUSTRALIA:** Adelaide (tel. 08/223-2426), Brisbane (tel. 07/221-9388), Cairns (tel. 070/314199), Darwin (tel. 089/412955), Melbourne (tel. 03/349-2411), Perth (tel. 09/227-7569), Sydney (tel. 02/212-1255). **FRANCE:** Paris (tel. 01-43-25-00-76). **NEW ZEALAND:** Auckland (tel. 09/309-9995), Christchurch (tel. 03/379-9098), Wellington (tel. 04/385-0561). **SPAIN:** Barcelona (tel. 03/487-9546), Madrid (tel. 01/541-7372). **UNITED KINGDOM:** London (tel. 0171/937-9962).

Travel **CUTS** is a full-service travel agency that sells discounted airline tickets to Canadian students and issues the ISIC, GO25, ITIC, and HI cards. Their 25 offices are on or near college campuses. Call weekdays 9–5 for info and reservations. *187 College St., Toronto, Ont. M5T 1P7, tel. 416/979–2406.*

HOSTELLING ORGANIZATIONS

Hostelling International (HI), also known as IYHF, is the umbrella group for a number of national youth hostel associations. HI offers single-sex dorm-style beds ("couples" rooms and family accommodations are available at many hostels) and self-service kitchen facilities at nearly 5,000 locations in more than 70 countries around the world (three in Paris, over 100 in France). Membership in any HI national hostel association (*see below*), open to travelers of all ages, allows you to stay in HI-affiliated hostels at member rates (about $10–$25 per night). Members also have priority if the hostel is full; they're eligible for discounts around the world, including rail and bus travel in some countries. The French division of Hostelling International is **Fédération Unie des Auberges de Jeunesse (FUAJ);** your HI card is good at all FUAJ hostels.

A one-year membership runs about $25 for adults (renewal $20) and $10 for those under 18. A one-night guest membership is about $3. Family memberships are available for $35, and a lifetime membership will set you back $250. Handbooks listing special discount opportunities (like budget cycling and hiking tours) are available from FUAJ and HI. There are also two international hostel directories: One covers Europe and the Mediterranean, while the other covers Africa, the Americas, Asia, and the Pacific ($13.95 each). Very useful is the HI web site (http://www.gnn.com/gnn/bus/ayh/index.html), which gives addresses and phone numbers for hostels all over the world and notes which ones will let you reserve in advance. *733 15th St. NW, Suite 840, Washington, D.C. 20005, tel. 202/783–6161.*

National branches of Hostelling International include **Hostelling International–American Youth Hostels** (HI–AYH, 733 15th St., Suite 840, Washington, D.C. 20005, tel. 202/783–6161); **Hostelling International–Canada** (HI–C, 400-205 Catherine St., Ottawa, Ont. K2P 1C3, tel. 613/237–7884 or 800/663-5777); **Youth Hostel Association of England and Wales** (YHA, Trevelyan House, 8 St. Stephen's Hill, St. Albans, Herts. AL1 2DY, England, tel. 01727/855–215); **Australian Youth Hostels Association** (YHA, Level 3, 10 Mallett St., Camperdown, New

The Highs and the Lows

Average daily temps (in degrees Fahrenheit) stack up as follows:

	Jan. Feb.	Mar. Apr.	May June	July Aug.	Sept. Oct.	Nov. Dec.
The Alps	41	55	71	79	65	44
Alsace-Lorraine	40	54	70	74	63	42
Brittany	49	55	65	71	66	53
Corsica	57	64	76	85	77	62
Loire Valley	45	57	71	78	66	47
Paris	44	56	70	76	65	46
Pyrénées	55	61	74	83	73	59
Riviera	56	61	72	82	73	61

The World At a Discount

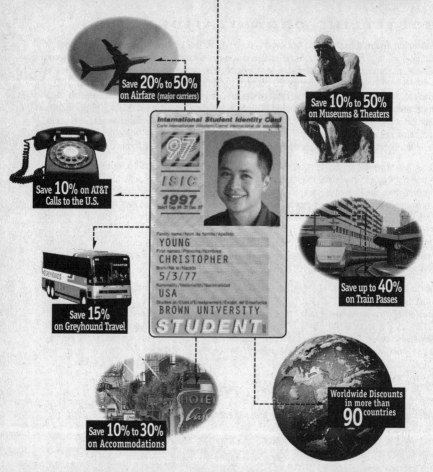

Save **20%** to **50%** on Airfare (major carriers)

Save **10%** to **50%** on Museums & Theaters

Save **10%** on AT&T Calls to the U.S.

International Student Identity Card
Carte internationale d'étudiant/Carnet internacional de estudiante

ISIC
1997

Family name/Nom de famille/Apellido
YOUNG
First names/Prénoms/Nombres
CHRISTOPHER
Born/Né le/Nacido
5/3/77
Nationality/Nationalité/Nacionalidad
USA
Studies at/Établd'Enseignement/Establ. de Enseñanza
BROWN UNIVERSITY
STUDENT

Save **15%** on Greyhound Travel

Save up to **40%** on Train Passes

Save **10%** to **30%** on Accommodations

Worldwide Discounts in more than **90** countries

The International Student Identity Card
Your Passport to Discounts & Benefits

With the ISIC, you'll receive discounts on airfare, hotels, transportation, computer services, foreign currency exchange, phone calls, major attractions, and more. You'll also receive basic accident and sickness insurance coverage when traveling outside the U.S. and access to a 24-hour, toll-free Help Line. Call now to locate the issuing office nearest you (over 555 across the U.S.) at:

Free 40-page handbook with each card!

1-888-COUNCIL (toll-free)

For an application and complete discount list, you can also visit us at **http://www.ciee.org/**

CIEE: Council on International Educational Exchange

South Wales 2050, tel. 02/565–1699); and **Youth Hostels Association of New Zealand** (YHA, Box 436, Christchurch 1, tel. 3/379–9970).

STUDENT ID CARDS

The **International Student Identity Card (ISIC)** entitles students to special fares on local transportation and discounts at museums, theaters, sports events, and other attractions. If the popular ISIC is purchased in the United States, the $19 cost also buys you $3,000 in emergency medical coverage; limited hospital coverage; and access to a 24-hour international, toll-free hot line for assistance in medical, legal, and financial emergencies. In the United States, apply to Council Travel or STA; in Canada, the ISIC is available for C$15 from Travel CUTS (see Budget Travel Organizations, above). In the United Kingdom, students with valid university IDs can purchase the ISIC at any student union or student-travel company. Applicants must submit a photo as well as proof of current full-time student status, age, and nationality.

The **Go 25: International Youth Travel Card (GO25)** is issued to travelers (students and non-students) between the ages of 12 and 25 and provides services and benefits similar to those given by the ISIC. The $19 card is available from the same organizations that sell the ISIC. When applying, bring a passport-size photo and your passport as proof of your age.

The **International Student Exchange Card (ISE),** is available to students and faculty members. You pay $18 and receive a $10 discount on flights within the United States and a $50 discount on certain flights to Europe. Write or call for more information or to enroll over the phone. *5010 E. Shea Blvd., Suite A104, Scottsdale, AZ 85254, tel. 602/951–1177 or 800/255–8000, fax 602/951–1216.*

The $20 **International Teacher Identity Card (ITIC),** sponsored by the International Student Travel Confederation, is available to teachers of all grade levels, from kindergarten to graduate school. With the ITIC you get benefits and services similar to those you get with the student cards. *The International Teacher Identity Card Handbook,* available when you buy the card, has all the details.

PASSPORTS AND VISAS

Although Brits need only a Visitor's Passport (a more restricted version of a passport) to enter France, everyone else needs a standard passport and possibly a visa. If you are an American, Canadian, or New Zealander, you need a visa only if you plan to stay in France longer than 90 days in a row or if you're enrolling in classes or working in France. Brits need a visa only if enrolling in classes. Australians need a visa for a visit of any length. Student visas are pretty easy to get; just apply a few weeks in advance. Long-stay and work visas, on the other hand, take several months to go through the system, so plan ahead. Contact the French consulate nearest you for more info. If you didn't *plan* to stay but just can't bear to leave your hostel in the mountains or your new French lover, contact the French immigration officials well before your three months are up.

OBTAINING A PASSPORT

➤ **U.S. CITIZENS** • First-time applicants, travelers whose most recent passport was issued more than 12 years ago or before they were 18, travelers whose passports have been lost or stolen, and travelers between the ages of 13 and 17 (a parent must also accompany them) must apply for a passport in person. Other renewals can be taken care of by mail. Apply at one of the 13 U.S. Passport Agency offices a *minimum* of five weeks before your departure. For fastest processing, apply between August and December. If you blow it, you can have a passport issued within five days of departure if you have your plane ticket in hand and pay the additional $30 fee to expedite processing. This method will probably work, but if there's one little glitch in the system, you're out of luck. Local county courthouses, many state and probate courts, and some post offices also accept passport applications. Have the following items ready when you go to get your passport:

MAXIMUM EUROPE. MINIMUM COST.

Flash your ISE Card to enjoy the best of Europe at discount prices!

Use your ISE Card to get a **$50.00 DISCOUNT off your overseas airline ticket plus $10.00 discount off domestic flights!** These discounts are off the lowest fare you can find—and you can use your ISE card to get the same discounts for your friends and family members too!

Use your ISE Card anywhere in Europe to SAVE UP TO 50% on...

- MUSEUM, CASTLE AND EXHIBITION ADMISSIONS
- STUDENT HOTEL RATES
- CONCERT, OPERA AND THEATER TICKETS
- TRAIN, BUS, FERRY TICKETS AND MORE!

Use your ISE Card to cover medical expenses! If you get sick or have an accident while traveling in Europe, we'll pay up to **$2,000** to cover the bills!

Use your ISE Card to get help when you need it—24 hours a day! Lose your passport or money? Need legal or medical help? No problem. Simply call ISE's toll-free Help Line to get instant assistance from one of our savvy professionals!

If you're a student, teacher or "youth" (non-student under age 26) you can enjoy the many benefits of an ISE Card for only $18 per year! Here's how to get your card...

Credit Card: Call toll-free 1-800-255-1000, Ext. 142 or access Internet http:\\\\www.Studentservices.com.

Check: Write to ISE Cards, Dept. 142, P.O. Box 22111, Phoenix, AZ 85028 (Include name, address, birth date, nationality and name of school)

International Student Exchange Cards

ise CARDS®

- A completed passport application (form DSP-11), available at courthouses, some post offices, and passport agencies.

- Proof of citizenship (certified copy of birth certificate, naturalization papers, or previous passport issued in the past 12 years).

- Proof of identity with your photograph and signature (for example, a valid driver's license, employee ID card, military ID, or student ID).

- Two recent, identical, 2-inch-square photographs (black-and-white or color head shots).

- A $55 application fee for a 10-year passport, $30 for those under 18 for a five-year passport. First-time applicants are also hit with a $10 surcharge. If you're paying cash, exact change is necessary; checks or money orders should be made out to Passport Services.

Those lucky enough to be able to renew their passports by mail must send a completed Form DSP-82 (available from a Passport Agency); two recent, identical passport photos; their current passport (less than 12 years old); and a check or money order for $55 ($30 if under 18). Send everything to the nearest Passport Agency. Renewals take from three to four weeks.

For more information or an application, contact the **Department of State Office of Passport Services** (tel. 202/647–0518) and dial your way through their message maze. Passport applications can be picked up at U.S. post offices, at federal or state courts, and at U.S. Passport Agencies in Boston, Chicago, Honolulu, Houston, Los Angeles, Miami, New Orleans, New York, Philadelphia, San Francisco, Seattle, Stamford, and Washington, D.C.

➤ **CANADIAN CITIZENS** • Canadians should send a completed passport application (available at any post office, passport office, and many travel agencies) to the **Bureau of Passports** (Suite 215, West Tower, Guy Favreau Complex, 200 René Levesque Boulevard W., Montréal, Qué. H2Z 1X4). Include C$60; two recent, identical passport photographs; the signature of a guarantor (a Canadian citizen who has known you for at least two years and is a mayor, practicing lawyer, notary public, judge, magistrate, police officer, signing officer at a bank, medical doctor, or dentist); and proof of Canadian citizenship (original birth certificate or other official document as specified). You can also apply in person at regional passport offices in many locations, including Edmonton, Halifax, Montréal, Toronto, Vancouver, and Winnipeg. Passports have a shelf life of five years and are not renewable. Processing takes about two weeks by mail and five working days for in-person applications. For more info call 514/283–2152.

➤ **U.K. CITIZENS** • Passport applications are available through travel agencies, a main post office, or one of six regional passport offices (in London, Liverpool, Peterborough, Belfast, Glasgow, and Newport). The application must be countersigned by your bank manager or by a solicitor, barrister, doctor, clergyman, or justice of the peace who knows you personally. Send or drop off the completed form; two recent, identical passport photos; and the £18 fee to a regional passport office (address is on the form). Passports are valid for 10 years (five years for those under 16) and take about four weeks to process. For more info, call the **Passport Office** (tel. 0171/279–4000; 0990/210–410 for recorded info).

➤ **AUSTRALIAN CITIZENS** • Australians must visit a post office or passport office to complete the passport application process. A 10-year passport for those over 18 costs AUS$81. The under-18 crowd can get a five-year passport for AUS$41. For more information, call toll-free in Australia 008/131–232 weekdays during regular business hours.

➤ **NEW ZEALAND CITIZENS** • Passport applications can be found at any post office or consulate. Completed applications must be accompanied by proof of citizenship and two passport-size photos. The fee is NZ$80 for a 10-year passport. Processing takes about 10 days.

LOST PASSPORTS If your passport is lost or stolen, you should immediately notify the local police and nearest embassy or consulate. It's going to be a pain to get a new one, so make a couple of copies, leave one at home, and carry the other with you separate from the originals. Better yet, give copies to your traveling companion. A consular officer should be able to wade through some red tape and issue you a new one, or at least get you back into your country of origin without one. The process will be slowed up considerably if you don't have some other forms of identification on you, so you're well advised to carry other forms of ID—a driver's license, a copy of your birth certificate, a student ID—separate from your passport.

A United States embassy or consulate will only issue a new passport in emergencies. In non-emergency situations, the staff will affirm your affidavit swearing to U.S. citizenship, and this paper will get you back into the United States. The British embassy or consulate requires a police report, any form of identification, and three passport-size photos. They will replace the passport in four working days. Canadian citizens face the same requirements as the Brits, but you must have a guarantor with you. Since most travelers do not know a local guarantor (for requirements *see* Obtaining a Passport, Canadian Citizens, *above*), there is also the option of paying an officer of the consulate/embassy to act in that capacity—proving that throwing money at a problem usually makes it go away. A replacement passport usually takes five working days. New Zealand officials ask for two passport-size photos, while the Australians require three, but both can usually replace a passport in 24 hours.

GETTING THE BEST AIRFARE DEALS

While your travel plans are still in the fantasy stage, start studying the travel sections of major newspapers: Courier services, charter companies, and fare brokers often list incredibly cheap flights. Travel agents are another obvious resource, as they have access to computer networks that show the lowest fares before they're even advertised. However, budget travelers are the bane of travel agents, whose commission is based on the ticket prices. That said, agencies on or near college campuses—try STA or Council Travel (*see* Budget Travel Organizations, *above*)—actually cater to this pariah class and can help you find cheap deals.

While a last-minute, round-trip ticket to Paris on Air France can cost $2,100 from New York and $2,400 from San Francisco, bargain-basement prices can go as low as $450. Flexibility is the key to getting a serious bargain on airfare. If you can play around with your departure date, destination, amount of luggage carried, and return date, you will probably save money. When setting travel dates, remember that off-season fares can be as much as 50% lower. Ask which days of the week are the cheapest to fly on—weekends are often the most expensive.

An extremely useful resource is Michael McColl's *The Worldwide Guide to Cheap Airfares,* an in-depth account of how to find cheap tickets and generally beat the system. The guide also includes a comprehensive listing of consolidators, charter companies, and courier services in budget-travel hub cities all over the world. If you don't find it at your local bookstore, you can mail a check for $14.95 plus $2.50 for shipping and handling to Insider Publications (2124 Kittredge St., 3rd Floor, Berkeley, CA 94704), or call 800/782–6657 and order with a credit card.

STUDENT DISCOUNTS Student discounts on airline tickets are offered through **Council,** the **Educational Travel Center, STA Travel,** and **Travel CUTS** (*see* Budget Travel Organizations, *above*). For discount tickets based on your status as a student, youth, or teacher, have an ID when you check in that proves it: an International Student Identity Card (ISIC), Youth Identity Card, or International Teacher Identity Card.

Campus Connection, exclusively for students under 25, searches airline computer networks for the cheapest student fares to worldwide destinations. They don't always have the best price, but because they deal with the airlines directly you won't get stuck with a heavily restricted or fraudulent ticket. *1100 E. Marlton Pike, Cherry Hill, NJ 08032, tel. 800/428–3235.*

CONSOLIDATORS AND BUCKET SHOPS Consolidator companies, also known as bucket shops, buy blocks of tickets at wholesale prices from airlines trying to fill flights. Check out any consolidator's reputation with the Better Business Bureau before starting; most are perfectly reliable, but better safe than sorry. Travel agents can also get you good consolidator fares and usually deal with respectable companies.

There are some drawbacks to the consolidator ticket: You can't always be too choosy about which city you fly into. Consolidator tickets are not always refundable, and the flights available will sometimes involve indirect routes, long layovers in connecting cities, and undesirable seating assignments. If your flight is delayed or canceled, you'll also have a tough time switching airlines. However, you can often find consolidator tickets that are changeable, with no minimum or maximum stays required, and these tickets are often a very good deal at the last minute. Bucket shops generally advertise in newspapers—be sure to check restrictions, refund possibilities, and payment conditions. If possible, pay with a credit card, so that if your ticket never arrives you don't have to pay. One last suggestion: Confirm your reservation with the airline both before and after you buy a consolidated ticket. This decreases the chance of fraud and ensures that you won't be the first to get bumped if the airline overbooks. For more details, contact one of the following consolidators.

Airfare Busters. *5100 Westheimer Ave., Suite 550, Houston, TX 77056, tel. 713/961–5109 or 800/232–8783, fax 713/961–3385.*

Globe Travel. *507 5th Ave., Suite 606, New York, NY 10017, tel. 800/969–4562, fax 212/682–3722.*

UniTravel. *1177 N. Warson Rd., Box 12485, St. Louis, MO 63132, tel. 314/569–2501 or 800/325–2222, fax 314/569–2503.*

Up & Away Travel. *347 Fifth Ave., Suite 202, New York, NY 10016, tel. 212/889–2345, fax 212/889–2350.*

CHARTER FLIGHTS Charter flights have vastly different characteristics, depending on the company you're dealing with. Generally speaking, a charter company either buys a block of tickets on a regularly scheduled commercial flight and sells them at a discount (the prevalent form in the United States) or leases the whole plane and then offers relatively cheap fares to the public (most common in the United Kingdom). Despite a few potential drawbacks—among them infrequent flights, restrictive return-date requirements, lickety-split payment demands, frequent bankruptcies—charter companies often offer the cheapest tickets around, especially during high season when other fares are most expensive. Make sure you find out a company's policy on refunds should a flight be canceled by either yourself or the airline. Summer charter flights fill up fast and should be booked a couple of months in advance.

You're in much better shape when the company is offering tickets on a regular commercial flight. After you've bought the ticket from the charter folks, you generally deal with the airline directly. When a charter company has chartered the whole plane, things get a little sketchier: Bankrupt operators, long delays at check-in, overcrowding, and flight cancellations are fairly common. Other charter troubles: weird departure times, packed planes, and a dearth of one-way tickets. Nevertheless, in peak season, charters are very often the cheapest way to go. You can minimize risks by checking the company's reputation with the Better Business Bureau.

Charter companies to try include **DER Tours** (Box 1606, Des Plains, IL 60017, tel. 800/782–2424), **MartinAir** (tel. 800/627–8462), **Tower Air** (tel. 800/34–TOWER), and **Travel CUTS** (187 College St., Toronto, Ont. M5T 1P7, tel. 416/979–2406). Council Travel and STA (*see* Budget Travel Organizations, *above*) also offer exclusively negotiated discount airfares on scheduled airlines.

COURIER FLIGHTS Courier flights are simple: You sign a contract with a courier service to baby-sit their packages (often without ever laying eyes on them, let alone hands), and the courier company pays half or more of your airfare. On the day of departure, you arrive at the airport a few hours early, meet someone who hands you a ticket and customs forms, and off you go. After you land, you simply clear customs with the courier luggage, and deliver it to a waiting agent.

Courier flights are cheap and easy, yes, but there are restrictions: 1) Flights can usually be booked only a week or two in advance and often only a few days in advance, (2) you are allowed carry-on luggage only, because the courier uses your checked-luggage allowance to transport the time-sensitive shipment, (3) you must return within one to four weeks, 4) times and destinations are limited, 5) you may be asked to pay a deposit, to be refunded after you have completed your assignment.

Find courier companies in the travel section of the newspaper or the yellow pages of your phone directory, or mail away for a telephone directory that lists companies by the cities to which they fly. One of the better publications is *Air Courier Bulletin* (IAATC, 8 South J St., Box 1349, Lake

Worth, FL 33460, tel. 407/582–8320), sent to IAATC members every two months once they pay the $45 annual fee. Publications you can find in bookstores include **Air Courier Bargains** ($14.95), published by The Intrepid Traveler, and **The Courier Air Travel Handbook** ($9.95), published by Thunderbird Press.

Now Voyager (tel. 212/431–1616) connects travelers scrounging for cheap airfares with companies looking for warm bodies to escort their packages overseas. Departures are from New York and Newark, and occasionally Los Angeles or Detroit; destinations may be in Europe, Asia, or Mexico (City, that is). Round-trip fares start at $150. A nonrefundable $50 registration fee, good for one year, is required. Call for current offerings.

LAST-MINUTE DEALS Flying standby is almost a thing of the past. The idea is to purchase an open ticket and wait for the next available seat on the next available flight to your chosen destination. Airlines themselves no longer offer standby tickets but some travel agencies do. Three-day-advance-purchase youth fares are open only to people under 25 and can only be purchased within three days of departure. Return flights must also be booked no more than three days prior to departure. If you meet the above criteria, expect 10%–50% savings on published fares. Some courier companies keep a last-minute list of travelers who are willing to fly at a moment's notice. Call around to see which do and how you can be listed.

There are also a number of brokers that specialize in discount and last-minute sales, offering savings on unsold seats on commercial carriers and charter flights, as well as tour packages. If you're desperate to get to Paris by Wednesday, try **Last Minute Travel Club** (tel. 617/267–9800).

RAIL PASSES

Rail passes are a great deal if you're planning to cover a lot of ground in a short period, and they certainly spare you the time waiting in lines to buy tickets. However, before plunking down hundreds of dollars on a pass, there are several issues to consider. First, add up the prices of the rail trips you plan. Some travel agents have a manual that lists ticket prices, or you can call **Rail Europe** (tel. 800/438–7245), **Railpass Express** (tel. 800/722–7151), or **DER Tours** (tel. 800/782–2424), three agencies that sell rail passes over the phone. If you're under 26, subtract about 30% from the prices quoted by Rail Europe or your travel agent; that's how much you can save by purchasing a BIJ ticket (*see* French Rail Passes, Discount Cards, *below*) in Europe.

If you decide that you'll save money with a rail pass, you have three options: some sort of **EurailPass, France Railpass,** or **InterRail Pass** (InterRail is available only to those who have lived in an EU country for longer than six months). If you're under 26 years of age on your first day of travel, it's always a better deal to get a youth pass of some sort (Europass Youth, Eurail Youth Flexipass, or Eurail Youthpass). Youth passes are valid for second-class travel only. If you're 26 or over on your first day of travel, you're not eligible for a youth pass and have to buy one of the (much more expensive) passes valid for first-class travel. For this reason, rail passes are often not such a good deal for people 26 and older; you might do better buying individual tickets, since that way you can travel more cheaply in second class.

Be sure to buy your rail pass before leaving the United States; though Eurail passes are available in some European discount travel agencies and major train stations, they're more expensive there. Also, if you have firm plans to visit Europe next year, consider buying your pass *this* year. Prices for Eurail passes generally rise on December 31, and your pass is valid as long as you start traveling within six months of the purchase date. The upshot is that a pass bought on December 30, 1997, can be activated as late as June 30, 1998. All the prices listed below are valid through December 30, 1996, after which you can expect a jump in rates.

Last warnings: Don't assume that your rail pass guarantees you a seat on every train. Seat reservations (tel. 08–36–35–35–35) are required on some trains, including all TGVs (*see* Getting Around, By Train, *below*). *Couchettes* (sleeping compartments) on overnight trains cost about 90F extra. Also note that many rail passes entitle you to free or reduced fares on some ferries (though you should still make seat reservations in advance).

FRENCH RAIL PASSES A **France Railpass** is valid within France for three days of travel within a one-month period. First-class passes go for $198, second-class for $160; added days (up to six allowed) cost $30 each for either class. The France Railpass isn't available once you arrive (in fact, it can't even be used by residents or citizens of France), so be sure to pick one up before leaving home. Another good deal is the **France Rail 'n Drive Pass**; for only a bit more than the plain ol' train pass, you get three days of train travel and two days of Avis car rental within one month. A second-class pass goes for $239, and you can add car days (up to six) for $44 each and rail days for $30 each (per person). You get unlimited mileage and can pick up and drop off the car anywhere in France at no extra charge (Avis has 520 agencies in France), so this might not be a bad deal for seeing out-of-the-way châteaux. Car-rental reservations must be made directly with Avis at least seven days in advance (tel. 800/331–1084 in U.S.), and drivers must be age 24 or older. Neither the France Rail nor the France Rail 'n Drive pass is valid for travel in Corsica.

➣ **DISCOUNT CARDS** • You can buy a **Carte Carrissimo** discount card only in France and only if you're between the ages of 12 and 25. Passes are good for a year and cost 189F for four

Cool Travel Web Sites

Is the Internet all it's cracked up to be, or is it the eight-track of the '90s? Though making reservations and purchasing air tickets on-line is neither as easy nor as cheap as the digerati would have you believe, it is possible to find a breadth of helpful and downright freaky travel info on the net. For pretrip destination research and planning, it really can't be beat. The following list of sites will get you going:

- *Shoestring Travel offers great info for the budget traveler, including cheap accommodations listings and loads of links to other budget travel sites. Other travelers contribute their experiences. URL: http://www.STRATPUB.com.*

- *Whether you're looking for a jazz club in Florence, or Tlingit theater performance in Juneau, Travelocity will get you there. With descriptions and reviews of restaurants, museums, shops, and sights in thousands of cities worldwide, it's got some of the best travel info on the net. Travelocity also offers travel-related bulletin boards and on-line chats. URL: http://www.travelocity.com.*

- *Teleport Travel is an on-line airfare browser and ticketing agency. It may be helpful for researching ticket prices, and they offer some consolidator tickets. Check out the travel resource library, with links to the World Health Organization, the Centers for Disease Control, and the Electronic Embassy. URL: http://www.teleportal.com.*

- *The crazy Aussie traveler who edits No Shitting in the Toilet dispenses advice and a weekly Top Ten, from "Bummer Boat Rides" to "Bum Steers by Travel Guide Books." The bulletin board is handy for tips on cheap deals, and NSITT offers links to other budget-travel sites. URL: http://www.magna.com.au/~nglobe/nsitt/gt/gt.html.*

- *Webfoot's Guide to France is a list of Internet sites covering French travel information, regional information, Minitel access, Astérix comics, cave paintings, and a French–English dictionary. You'd be crazy not to check out this site before your trip. URL: http://www.webfoot.com/travel/guides/france/france.html.*

one-way trips, 295F for eight trips. Calendars given out with train tickets are color coded to indicate different fare periods; with the Carrissimo, you get 50% off on blue days (*période bleue*) and 20% off on white days (*période blanche*). This discount card is good for small groups, since the discount applies to up to three other people traveling with you—just be sure to stamp the card, along with your tickets, one time for each person using it. If you're over 21 with a valid driver's license, Avis will give you a 20% discount with the card for cars rented from the train station.

Similar to the Carte Carrissimo, the **Carte Vermeil** gives people over age 60 two discount options. The first costs 143F and follows the same rules as the four-trip Carrissimo listed above; the second is 270F and allows an unlimited number of reduced-price trips within France and a 30% discount on trips outside of France for one year. With the **Carte Kiwi** (285F for four trips; 444F for an unlimited number of trips), up to four children under 16 accompanying an adult can get a 50% discount for a full year. Married couples (you have to have a copy of your marriage certificate and one passport photo per person) can get the **Carte Couple** for free, which gives a 25% discount when traveling together in either class, although you can only travel in blue periods. If you know how to plan in advance, lower prices are also available by purchasing **Joker** (no joke) tickets up to two months before the date of departure (Joker 30, at least one month before, gives the best discount, while Joker 8, at least eight days before, allows you to indulge your slacker side). Joker deals are available on some international destinations as well.

If you don't actually want a rail pass, you might want to consider a **Billet International de Jeunesse** (International Youth Ticket), usually known as a **BIJ** or **BIGE** ticket. Here's how it works: Travelers under the age of 26 can purchase a second-class ticket between two far-flung European cities at a 20%–30% savings and then make unlimited stops along the way for up to two months. BIJ tickets are available throughout Europe at budget travel agencies; try the European offices of STA and Council Travel (*see* Budget Travel Organizations, *above*).

EURAIL The **EurailPass** is valid for unlimited first-class train travel through 17 countries—Austria, Belgium, Denmark, Finland, France, Germany, Greece, Hungary, Italy, Luxembourg, the Netherlands, Norway, Portugal, the Republic of Ireland, Spain, Sweden, and Switzerland. It's available for periods of 15 days ($522), 21 days ($678), one month ($838), two months ($1,148), and three months ($1,468). If you're under 26, the **Eurail Youthpass** is a much better deal. One or two months of unlimited second-class train travel costs $598 or $768, respectively. For 15 consecutive days of travel you pay $418.

A **Eurail Saverpass,** which costs a little less than a comparable EurailPass, is intended for couples and small groups. A pass good for 15 days of first-class travel is $452, for 21 days $578, for one month $712. The pass requires that a minimum of two people each buy a Saverpass and travel together at all times. Between April 1 and September 30 there is a three-person minimum.

Unlike the EurailPass and Eurail Youthpass, which are good for unlimited travel for a certain period of time, the **Eurail Flexipass** allows you to travel for 10 or 15 days within a two-month period. The Flexipass is valid in the same 17 countries as the EurailPass and costs $616 for 10 days, $812 for 15 days. If you're under 26, the second-class **Eurail Youth Flexipass** is a better deal. Within a two-month period it entitles you to 10 ($438) or 15 ($588) days of travel.

For travel in France, Germany, Italy, Spain, and Switzerland, consider the **Europass** (first-class) or **Europass Youth** (second-class). The basic Europass is good for five, six, or seven days of travel in any three of the above-named countries, as long as they border one another. The five-day pass costs $316 (first-class) or $210 (second-class). The eight-, nine- and 10-day passes are good in four of the five countries. The eight-day pass costs $442 (first-class) or $297 (second-class). The passes, good for any number of days from 11 to 15, are valid in all five countries. The 11-day pass costs $568 (first-class) or $384 (second-class). In all cases the days of travel can be spread out over two calendar months. Call Rail Europe or ask a travel agent for the brochures "1997 Europe On Track" or "EurailPass and Europass" for details on adding extra travel days, buying a discounted pass for your companion, or expanding the reach of your pass to Austria, Belgium, Greece, Luxembourg, and Portugal.

➢ **PASS VALIDATION AND INSURANCE** • The very first time you use any Eurail pass you must have it validated. Before getting on the train, go to a ticket window and have the agent fill out the necessary forms—a painless but important procedure that could save you being asked to get off the train or being fined. Also, you might want to consider Eurail's "Pass Protection Plan," which costs $10 and must be arranged at the time of purchase. If you bought the protection plan and your pass mysteriously disappears, file a police report within 24 hours and keep the receipts for any train tickets you purchase. Then, upon your return home, send a copy of the report and receipts to Eurail. For your trouble you get a 100% refund on the *unused* portion of your stolen or lost pass.

INTERRAIL European citizens and anyone who has lived in the EU for at least six months can purchase an **InterRail Pass,** valid for 15 days' travel in one zone (1,428F) or one month's travel in two or more zones (1,700F and up). One month's travel in all of the zones will set you back 2,142F. The passes work much like Eurail, except that you only get a 50% reduction on train travel in the country where it was purchased. Be prepared to prove EU citizenship or six months of continuous residency. In most cases you'll have to show your passport for proof of age and residency, but sometimes they'll accept a European university ID. To prove residency, old passport entry stamps may do the trick, but be forewarned that each time passes are presented, the ticket controller has the option of looking at passports and confiscating "illegitimate" passes. InterRail can only be purchased in Europe at rail stations and some budget travel agencies; try the European branches of STA or Council Travel (*see* Budget Travel Organizations, *above*).

MONEY

The units of currency in France are the franc and the centime (1 franc = 100 centimes). Bills come in denominations of 20, 50, 100, 200, and 500 francs. Coins are worth ½, 1, 2, 5, 10, and 20 francs and 5, 10, and 20 centimes. Try to familiarize yourself with the look of the 10F coin; some bozo counterfeited it, and French salespeople are all too eager to dump the fake version on tourists. When you plan your budget, allow for fluctuating exchange rates; at press time, the exchange rate for the French franc was:

U.S.	Canada	Britain	Australia	New Zealand
$1 = 4F96	C$1 = 3F62	£1 = 7F68	AUS$1 = 3F93	NZ$1 = 3F41
1 F = 20¢	1F = 27¢	1F = 13p	1F = 25¢	1F = 29¢

The French use two methods of listing prices that include centimes. While 5 francs is always 5F, a price of 4 francs and 70 centimes may be rendered either 4F70 or 4,70F. In all our price listings we use the first method.

HOW MUCH IT WILL COST It's hard to say how much money you need to travel in France. Some people are happy sleeping in dirtbag hotels, while others can't live without cushy carpeting and sanitized toilet seats. Assuming you fall somewhere in the middle, you can stay in France for about $50 a day (plus transportation expenses), less if you're really frugal, more if you want to splurge.

➢ **LODGING** • While hostels may be the best deal for solo travelers, those traveling in twos or threes can do just as well splitting a hotel room. Doubles usually start around 120F. Campgrounds charge anywhere between 30F and 80F per person.

➢ **FOOD** • Though you can survive quite well on fresh produce, cheese, and bread bought at outdoor markets or grocery stores, sitting down in a French restaurant for a multicourse meal at least once is a moral imperative. A three-course dinner will run you at least 70F, though the same meal will cost substantially less (maybe 50F) at lunchtime.

➢ **ENTERTAINMENT** • This is where you go broke fast. Cover charges for nightclubs range from 70F to 140F and usually include one drink. Drinks in clubs are outrageously expensive—about 50F each. A beer in a bar goes for 12F–20F. Movies are pretty expensive (about 40F), but discount tickets are often sold for around 30F for students or on certain days of the week (often Wednesdays), and always for matinées. Classical music and theater are about as expensive as elsewhere, with student and rush tickets available.

➢ **TIPPING** • Service is included at restaurants, cafés, and brasseries, and it's 100% normal not to leave a centime. If you love the service though, or someone called you a cab, then leave anywhere from 2F to 10F. In the case of taxi drivers and hairdressers, tip 10%. At the airport, avoid paying luggage porters by getting your own cart. Ushers who help opera- and theater-goers to their seats should receive a tip of around 5F.

TRAVELING WITH MONEY A major U.S. credit card (especially Visa, known in France as Carte Bleue) with accompanying personal identification number (PIN) is often the safest and most convenient way to pay for goods and services in Paris and larger towns; many hotels, restaurants, and shops accept credit cards, and you'll find numerous ATMs that will give you money at favorable exchange rates (*see* Getting Money from Home, *below*). Traveler's checks also come in handy. While few merchants accept them in foreign currencies, you can exchange them for cash at many banks and almost all bureaux de change. Whichever method you use, protect yourself by carrying cash in a money belt or "necklace" pouch, and by keeping records of your credit card numbers and traveler's check serial numbers in a few safe places.

You'll get a better deal buying French francs in France than at your bank in Australia or the States. Nevertheless, it's a good idea to exchange a bit of money into francs before you arrive in France in case the exchange booth at the train station or airport at which you arrive is closed.

CHANGING MONEY You lose money every time you exchange currency, so try to exchange larger chunks of money; no point spending the first half of each morning looking for a place with good rates. At the same time, you don't want to change so much money that you have to exchange it back when you leave the country. The best place to exchange your cash or traveler's checks for francs varies, though, generally speaking, the Banque de France has good rates. Private exchange offices will occasionally have better rates—just watch out for commissions, which can run up to 5%. It helps to exchange money during regular business hours when you have the greatest number of options.

TRAVELER'S CHECKS An increasingly outmoded form of currency in the face of ATMs, traveler's checks can be transformed into cash at banks, some hotels, tourist offices, AmEx offices, or currency-exchange offices. AmEx checks are the most widely accepted; other brands are sometimes refused. Some banks and credit unions will issue checks free to established customers, but most charge a 1%–2% commission fee. The reward for paying this commission is being able to get your money back if some nimble-fingered thief takes off with your checks (*see* Lost and Stolen Checks, *below*). If you want to gamble on your country's currency weakening during your vacation, buy traveler's checks in French francs, which all banks in France must cash at face value (no commission)—they're also generally accepted for larger purchases and at small hotels that don't have bureaux de change. Just don't forget that any checks left over will have to be re-exchanged on your return home.

American Express card members can order traveler's checks in U.S. dollars and some foreign currencies by phone, free of charge (with a gold card) or for a 1% commission (with your basic green card). In three to five business days you'll receive your checks: Up to $1,000 can be ordered in a seven-day period. Checks can also be purchased through many banks, in which case both gold and green cardholders pay a 1% commission. AmEx also issues **Traveler's Cheques for Two,** checks that can be signed and used by either you or your traveling companion. If you lose your checks or are ripped off, true to Karl Malden's repeated pledges, AmEx has the resources to provide you with a speedy refund—often within 24 hours. At their Travel Services offices (about 1,500 around the world) you can usually buy and cash traveler's checks, write a personal check in exchange for traveler's checks, report lost or stolen checks, exchange foreign currency, and pick up mail. *Tel. 800/221–7282 in U.S. and Canada.*

Citicorp traveler's checks are available from Citibank and other banks worldwide in U.S. dollars and some foreign currencies. For 45 days from date of check purchase, purchasers have access to the 24-hour International S.O.S. Assistance Hotline, which can provide English-speaking doctor, lawyer, and interpreter referrals; assistance with loss or theft of travel documents; traveler's check refund assistance; and an emergency message center. *Tel. 800/645-6556 in U.S. or 813/623-1709 collect outside U.S.*

Thomas Cook issues **MasterCard International** traveler's checks, available in U.S. dollars and several foreign currencies. If purchased through a Thomas Cook Foreign Exchange office (formerly Deak International), no extra charge is levied to get traveler's checks in French francs. There are over 100 Thomas Cook exchange offices/travel agencies throughout France; call them for a brochure that tells you where they are. *Tel. 800/223-7373 in U.S.; in Europe, tel. 447/335-02-995 toll-free or 07/335-02-995 collect.*

Visa traveler's checks are available in U.S. dollars and British pounds. *Tel. 800/227-6811 in U.S. and Canada; outside the U.S.Check local listings outside the U.S.*

➤ **LOST AND STOLEN CHECKS** • Unlike cash, lost or stolen traveler's checks can be replaced or refunded *if you* can produce the purchase agreement and a record of the checks' serial numbers. Common sense dictates that you keep the purchase agreement separate from your checks. Caution-happy travelers will even give a copy of the purchase agreement and checks' serial numbers to someone back home. Most issuers of traveler's checks promise to refund or replace lost or stolen checks in 24 hours, but you can practically see them crossing their fingers behind their backs. If you are traveling in a remote area, expect this process to take longer. In a safe place—or several safe places—record the toll-free or collect telephone number to call in case of emergencies (*see above*).

If you don't have an AmEx gold card, you can still get American Express traveler's checks free with an AAA membership. Talk to the cashier at your local AAA office.

CREDIT CARDS Many restaurants, cafés, bars, shops, and hotels will accept credit cards with a 100F minimum—look for the card logo on windows. Also keep in mind that any place that accepts the French card Carte Bleu also accepts Visa. MasterCard and Visa, but not always American Express, can be used at many banks and ATMs to get a cash advance (*see* Cash Machines, *below*).

Even if you have no job, no credit, no cards, and no respect, you can still tap into services offered by the **Visa Assistance Center** if one of your parents has a Visa Gold or Business card and you are a dependent of 22 years or less and at least 100 miles from home. Write down the card number in a safe place and call the center for emergency cash service, emergency ticket replacement, lost-luggage assistance, medical and legal assistance, and an emergency message service. Helpful, multilingual personnel await your call 24 hours a day, seven days a week. *Tel. 800/847-2911 in U.S. or 410/581-3836 collect from Europe.*

GETTING MONEY FROM HOME

Provided there is money at home to be had, there are at least six ingenious ways to get it:

- Have it sent through a large **commercial bank** that has a branch or sister bank wherever you are. Unless you have an account with that large bank, though, you'll have to initiate the transfer at your own bank, and the process will be even slower and more expensive.

- If you're an **American Express** cardholder, cash a personal check at an AmEx office for up to $1,000 ($2,500 for gold cardholders) every 21 days; you'll be paid in U.S. traveler's checks or, if you want, in foreign currency.

- The **MoneyGram**^{SM} service is a dream *if* you can convince someone back home to go to a MoneyGram agent and fill out the necessary forms. Simply pay up to $1,000 with a credit card or cash (and anything over that in cash) and, as quickly as 10 minutes later, it's ready to be picked up. Fees vary according to the amount of money sent, but average about 8% to send money from the United States to France. You have to show ID when picking up the money if you're receiving more than $900. For locations of MoneyGram agents call 800/926-9400; from overseas call 303/980-3340 collect.

Stuck for cash? Don't panic. With Western Union, money is transferred to you in minutes. It's easy. All you've got to do is ask someone at home to give Western Union a call on US 1 800 3256000. Minutes later you can collect the cash.

WESTERN UNION | MONEY TRANSFER®

The fastest way to send money worldwide.

- Take your **Visa, MasterCard,** or **American Express** card to an ATM machine and hope for the best. For more information, *see* Cash Machines, *below*.

- Have funds sent through **Western Union** (tel. 800/325–6000). If you have a MasterCard or Visa, you can have money sent up to your card's credit limit. If not, have someone take cash, a certified cashier's check, or a healthy MasterCard or Visa to a Western Union office. The money will reach the requested destination in minutes, but it may not be available for several more hours or days, depending on the whim of local authorities. Fees range from about 5% to 15%, depending on the amount sent.

- In extreme emergencies (arrest, hospitalization, or worse) there is one more way American citizens can receive money overseas: by setting up a **Department of State Trust Fund.** A friend or family member sends money to the Department of State, which then transfers the money to the U.S. embassy or consulate in the city in which you're stranded. Once this account is established, you can send and receive money through Western Union, bank wire, or mail, all payable to the Department of State. For information, talk to the Department of State's Citizens' Emergency Center (tel. 202/647–5225).

CASH MACHINES Virtually all U.S. banks belong to a network of card-slurping, cash-expectorating ATMs. Some are affiliated with the **Cirrus** and **Plus** systems, some with **Exchange,** some with **Star.** In theory, this is the best way to get money; in practice, your card may only work sporadically, so when it does, withdraw as much as you think safe to carry. If you can convince a machine to take your card, this is the best way to get francs at the excellent commercial exchange rate, and the transaction fees may be lower than the interest charged by your credit card for cash withdrawals. Just make sure you have a back-up method of getting money.

To increase your chances of happy encounters with cash machines, take a few precautions *before* you go. ATMs in France accept PINs of four or fewer digits only; if your PIN is longer, ask your bank at home about changing it. If you know your PIN as a word, learn the numerical equivalent before you leave, since most French ATM keypads show numbers only, no letters. Foreign ATMs still abide by the withdrawal limits set for you by your bank at home, so make a rough estimate of that amount in French francs and round down to the nearest 100F. Many American banks will waive transaction fees for other-bank ATM use for the duration of lengthy trips; show them your plane ticket and ask nicely *before* you go.

Outside Paris, however, the quest for after-hour ATMs might put the unprepared tourist in a bind. Cash machines on the Cirrus or Plus systems are often nonexistent. To find out if there are any cash machines in a given city, call your bank's department of international banking. Or call **Cirrus** (tel. 800/424–7787) for a list of worldwide locations. **Plus** also has a toll-free number (tel. 800/843–7587) but only lists ATMs in the U.S. and Canada; if you're calling from Europe for information on ATMs, call collect 410/581–9994.

A **Visa** or **MasterCard** can also be used to access cash through certain ATMs (provided you have a PIN for it), but the fees for this service are usually higher than bank-card fees. Also, a daily interest charge usually begins to accrue immediately on these credit card "loans," even if monthly bills are paid up. Check with your bank for information on fees and on the daily limit for cash withdrawals.

Express Cash allows AmEx cardholders to withdraw up to $1,000 in a seven-day period (21 days overseas) from their personal checking accounts via a worldwide network of ATMs. Gold cardholders can receive up to $2,500 in a seven-day period (21 days overseas). Each transaction carries a 2% fee, with a minimum charge of $2.50 and a maximum of $20. Apply for a PIN and set up the linking of your accounts at least two to three weeks before departure. Call 800/528–4800 for an application.

WHAT TO PACK

As little as possible. Besides the usual suspects—clothes, toiletries, camera, a Walkman, and a good book—bring along a day pack; it'll come in handy not only for day excursions but also for those places where you plan to stay for only one or two days. You can check heavy, cum-

The trouble with "reliable travel gear" is that it's so hard to find

Hint: Call 1-800-688-9577 for a FREE catalog

We're in the "reliable travel gear" business. We have a variety of backpacks, and over 100 exciting products in this year's catalog to make your trip safe, comfortable, and easy.

The **Eagle Creek Continental Journey backpack** is just one of those products. This tough high quality travel pack features 3,900 cubic inches of storage for your clothing and gear. It even includes a zip-off day pack! You can carry the entire unit as a shoulder bag or unzip the hidden shoulder straps to haul as a backpack. Top and side handles make it ideal for getting on and off of trains. The main compartment is large enough to live out of, but still meets most airline "carry-on" limits.

EURAIL PASSES are available for 1997! We can help you select the right pass for your journey. We'll even include a <u>free</u> rail guide with valuable information about your pass.

And there's more. If you're looking for a **money belt** (shown below), **film protector, sleep sack, or even laundry gear**, we have what you need! Look our catalog over, it's free. Call now 1-800-688-9577.

J15 Eagle Creek Continental Journey Backpack $149

Most orders are shipped within 24 hours anywhere in the U.S.A.

Call anytime day or night 1-800-688-9577. Just leave your name and address, and we'll send you a catalog immediately, or visit us at our web site www.brtravelgear.com.

C32 Money Belt $10.50

Bitter Root Travel Gear
P.O. Box 3538, Dana Point, CA 92629

www.brtravelgear.com or call **1-800-688-9577**

bersome bags at the train or bus station (or leave it at your hotel) and just carry the essentials while you are out and about.

BEDDING Hostels require that you use a sleep sheet. Some include them in the price, some rent them, and some don't. If you have a backpack, consider bringing a sleeping mat too; it can be rolled tightly and strapped onto the bottom of your pack.

THE SLEEP SHEET:
Take a big sheet (flannel sheets are great for this). Fold it down the middle the long way. Sew one short side and the long, open side. Turn inside out. Get inside. Sleep.

CLOTHING Smart—and not terribly fashion-conscious— travelers will bring two outfits and learn to wash their clothes by hand. At the very least, bring comfortable, easy-to-clean clothes. Black hides dirt but also absorbs heat. Artificial fabrics don't breathe and will make you hotter than you'd thought possible, so go with light cotton instead. Bring several T-shirts and a sweater for cooler nights. Shorts will almost certainly brand you as a foreigner in France. The French dress more formally than Americans, so plan on bringing your nicest traveling clothes if you don't want people staring at your tennis shoes and tie-dye T-shirt.

A sturdy pair of walking shoes or hiking boots (broken in before your trip) and a spare pair (probably sandals) allow you to switch off and give your dogs a rest. Plastic sandals or thongs protect feet on hostile shower floors and are also useful camping or beach hopping. If you're planning on hitting the nightclubs, you'll need something nicer than tennis shoes or thongs.

ELECTRONIC STUFF Before tossing a blow-dryer into your bag, consider that European electrical outlets pump out 220 volts, enough to fry American appliances. If you absolutely must have your electric toothbrush, you need a converter that matches your appliance's wattage and the outlet's current. In addition to taking up precious packing space, a converter costs about $20 and is not necessarily reliable in older hotels with bad sockets.

LAUNDRY Hotel rooms are the best place (certainly the cheapest) to do laundry. A bring-your-own laundry service includes a plastic bottle of liquid detergent (powder doesn't break down as well), about six feet of clothesline, and some plastic clips (bobby pins or paper clips can substitute). When faced with a plugless sink, stuff a sock or plastic bag in the drain. Be sure to bring a few extra plastic bags for damp laundry and dirty clothes.

TOILETRIES Use containers that seal tightly and pack them in a separate, waterproof bag; the pressure on airplanes can cause lids to pop off and create instant moisturizer slicks inside your luggage. Bring all the paraphernalia you need to conduct chemical warfare on your contact lenses if you wear them. Tampons (overpriced), deodorant, soap, shampoo, and toothpaste can all be bought in France, but you should bring any prescription drugs you might need. Bring your own birth control; condoms are expensive (at least 5F each), and you probably don't know the French word for "dental dam."

MISCELLANEOUS Stuff you might not think to take but will be damn glad to have: (1) a flashlight, good for reading in the dark and exploring wine cellars; (2) a pocket knife for cutting fruit, spreading cheese, removing splinters, and opening bottles; (3) a water bottle; (4) a first-aid kit; (5) sunglasses; (6) several large zip-type plastic bags, useful for wet swimsuits, towels, leaky bottles, and rancid socks; (7) a travel alarm clock; (8) a needle and small spool of thread; (9) extra batteries; (10) a few good books; (11) ketchup packets (they make you pay extra for it in French fast-food joints).

STAYING HEALTHY

There are few serious health risks associated with travel in France, and no inoculations are needed to enter the country. If you get diarrhea, it's probably from upping your wine and rich food intake, not from a bacterial infection. Tap water is drinkable everywhere, but it won't hurt you to know that *eau non potable* means non-drinkable water.

HEALTH AND ACCIDENT INSURANCE Some general health insurance plans cover health expenses incurred while traveling, so review your existing health policies (or a parent's policy, if you're a dependent) before leaving home. Most university health insurance plans begin and end with the school year, so don't count on school spirit to pull you through. Canadian travelers should check with their provincial ministry of health to see if their resident health insurance plan covers them on the road.

Organizations such as STA and Council (*see* Budget Travel Organizations, *above*), as well as some credit-card conglomerates, include health-and-accident coverage with the purchase of an ID or credit card. If you purchase an ISIC card you're automatically insured for $100 a day for in-hospital sickness expenses, up to $3,000 for accident-related medical expenses, and $25,000 for emergency medical evacuation. For details, request a summary of coverage from Council (205 East 42nd St., New York, NY 10017, tel. 888/COUNCIL, http://www.ciee.org). Council Travel and STA also offer inexpensive short-term insurance coverage designed specifically for the budget traveler. Otherwise, several private companies offer coverage designed to supplement existing health insurance for travelers; for more details contact your favorite student travel organization or one of the agencies listed below.

Carefree Travel Insurance covers emergency medical evacuation and accidental death or dismemberment. It also offers 24-hour medical phone advice. Basic coverage for an individual ranges from $86 for a 30-day trip to $180 for a 90-day trip. Deluxe coverage is about twice that. *100 Garden City Plaza, Box 9366, Garden City, NY 11530, tel. 516/294–0220 or 800/323–3149.*

International SOS Assistance offers insurance through Insure America, providing emergency evacuation services, medical reports on your destination, worldwide medical referrals, and medical and trip-cancellation insurance. If all else fails, they also cover the return of "mortal remains." *Box 11568, Philadelphia, PA 19116, tel. 215/244–1500 or 800/523–8930.*

Travel Guard offers a variety of insurance plans, many of which are endorsed by the American Society of Travel Agents. A basic plan, including medical coverage and emergency assistance, starts at $53 for a five-day trip. Trip-cancellation policies are available for as little as $19. *1145 Clark St., Stevens Point, WI 54481, tel. 715/345–0505 or 800/782–5151.*

Wallach & Company offers two comprehensive medical insurance plans, both covering hospitalization, surgery, office visits, prescriptions, and medical evacuation for as little as $3 per day. Both also buy you access to a network of worldwide assistance centers that are staffed 24 hours a day by English speakers. *107 W. Federal St., Box 480, Middleburg, VA 20118, tel. 800/237–6615, fax 540/687–3172.*

MEDICAL ASSISTANCE International Association for Medical Assistance to Travellers (IAMAT) offers free membership (donations are much appreciated) and entitles you to a worldwide directory of qualified English-speaking physicians who are on 24-hour call and who have agreed to a fixed-fee schedule. *United States: 417 Center St., Lewiston, NY 14092, tel. 716/754–4883. Canada: 40 Regal Rd., Guelph, Ont. N1K 1B5, tel. 519/836–0102. Switzerland: 57 Voirets, 1212 Grand-Lancy-Geneva. New Zealand: Box 5049, Christchurch 5.*

British travelers can join **Europe Assistance Worldwide Services** (252 High St., Croyden, Surrey CRO 1NF, tel. 0181/680–1234) to gain access to a 24-hour, 365-day-a-year telephone hotline that can help in a medical emergency. The American branch of this organization is **Worldwide Assistance Incorporated** (1133 15th St. NW, Suite 400, Washington, D.C. 20005, tel. 800/821–2828), which offers emergency evacuation services and 24-hour medical referrals. An individual membership costs $62 for up to 15 days, $164 for 60 days. Families may purchase coverage for $92 for 15 days, $234 for 60 days.

Diabetic travelers should contact the **American Diabetes Association** (1660 Duke St., Alexandria, VA 22314, tel. 703/549–1500 or 800/232–3472) or the **Canadian Diabetes Association** (15 Toronto St., Suite 1001, Toronto, Ont. M5C 2E3, tel. 416/363–3373) for resources and medical referrals. *The Diabetic Traveler* (Box 8223, Stamford, CT 06905, tel. 203/327–5832), published four times a year, lists vacations geared toward diabetics and offers travel and medical advice. Subscriptions are $18.95. An informative article entitled "Management of Diabetes During Intercontinental Travel," a listing of diabetic associations, and an insulin adjustment card are available for free.

PRESCRIPTIONS Bring as much as you need of any prescription drugs (*ordonnance* in French), as well as your written prescription (packed separately). Ask your doctor to *type* the prescription and include the dosage, the generic name, and the manufacturer's name. To avoid problems clearing customs, diabetic travelers carrying syringes should have handy a letter from their physician confirming their need for insulin injections.

Most pharmacies close at 7 or 8 PM, but the *commissariat de police* in every city has a list of the *pharmacies de garde,* the pharmacists on call (literally, on guard) for the evening. This is an emergency-only service, and you may have to go to (as opposed to just call) the commissariat in order to get the name. Pharmacies de garde are also sometimes listed in newspapers or posted on the doors of closed pharmacies.

CONTRACEPTIVES AND SAFE SEX AIDS (in French, *SIDA*) and other *maladies sexuelle-ment transmissibles* (*MST,* or sexually transmitted diseases) do not respect national boundaries; protect yourself when you travel as you would at home. If you're planning a rendezvous and have neglected to bring *un préservatif* (condom) from home, pick some up at a French pharmacy. You won't find nonoxynol-9 versions here, though; sales were discontinued several years ago. However, women can add to condoms' effectiveness with *ovules* (spermicidal vaginal suppositories).

Condoms are available in dispensers outside many pharmacies for your late-night needs. In general, though, you'll have a hard time finding contraceptives in stores other than pharmacies. Condoms cost about 10F for two, 49F for a box of 12. Women should bring any birth control from home, because it may be difficult to find the exact equivalent in France. If you forget your prescription for *la pillule* (the Pill), a sympathetic pharmacist may forgo the formality, but the side effects of the switch to a French version may be such that you wish he or she hadn't. IUDs and diaphragms are available, but you have to see a doctor to get fitted, and it's hardly the sort of thing you'd want to do on a vacation. Pack condoms or diaphragms in a pouch or case where they will not become squashed or damaged. If all of the above fails and the *test de grossesse* (pregnancy test) from the pharmacy is positive, your options in France are limited: Given the more conservative political climate of late, abortion services are now legally available only to women who can prove they've been living in France for at least six months.

CRIME AND PUNISHMENT

DRINKING AND DRIVING The legal blood alcohol level for drivers has recently been reduced from 0.7% to 0.5%. To the frustration of the wine-loving French, this is the equivalent of about two glasses of wine for most drinkers.

DRUGS Many young French are tolerant (even enthusiastic) about drug use. Heroin, LSD, MDMA, amphetamines, cocaine, and marijuana are all bought and sold here. Drug possession and consumption, however, are punishable by hefty fines. Drug *selling* is also big no-no—if you're caught, you'll go to jail for sure. If you get busted for drugs (or breaking any other law), your embassy might say a few sympathetic words but cannot give you one iota of legal help. You're on your own. But just in case you were wondering: *la came/la dope* (hard drugs), *la poudre/le drepou* (heroin), *l'extasie/des x* (ecstasy), *l'acide* (LSD), *le teuch/le chit* (hashish), *l'herbe/la beuh* (marijuana), *un pétard* (a joint).

PROTECTING YOUR VALUABLES Money belts may be dorky and bulky, but it's better to be embarrassed than broke. You'd be wise to carry all cash, traveler's checks, credit cards, and your passport in an inaccessible place: front or inner pocket, a bag that fits underneath your clothes, or even in your shoes. Keep a copy of your passport somewhere else, as it will be the biggest pain to replace. Neck pouches and money belts are sold in luggage and camping-supply stores. Waist packs are safe if you keep the pack part in front of your body, safer still if your shirt or sweater hangs over the pack. And it goes without saying, but *never* leave your pack unguarded, not even if you're only planning to be gone for a minute.

RESOURCES FOR WOMEN

Although times are changing, the idea still exists that women traveling alone are fair game for lewd comments, leering looks, and the like. Harassment is usually verbal—always annoying, but not often violent. *Dragueurs* (men who persistently profess their undying love to hapless female passersby) tend to be very vocal, especially in large cities. But the threat they pose is no greater than in any big city back home.

There are precautions you can take to avoid some harassment. Dressing conservatively helps; think about the area you're in before putting on that short skirt or tight body suit. Walk with a deliberate step and don't be afraid to show your irritation. Avoiding eye contact and conversation with potential sleazeballs also helps. Finally, be aware of your surroundings and use your head; don't do things abroad that you wouldn't do at home. Hitchhiking alone, for example, is not the brightest idea, nor is walking back to your hotel at night along deserted streets. If you get into an uncomfortable situation, move into a public area and make your fear widely known.

PUBLICATIONS Major travel publications for women include *Women Travel: Adventures, Advice, and Experience* ($12.95), published by Prentice Hall. More than 70 countries receive some sort of coverage in the form of journal entries and short articles. As far as practical travel information goes, it offers few details on prices, phone numbers, and addresses. The *Handbook for Women Travelers* ($14.95) by Maggie and Gemma Moss has some very good info on women's health and personal safety while traveling. For a nice companion book, look for *Maiden Voyages* ($14), edited by Mary Morris and published by Vintage Books. This collection of travel writings by women includes everyone from Mary Wollstonecraft to Joan Didion. All of these books should be available at any bookstore, or have your local shop order them for you.

ORGANIZATIONS Headquartered in Paris is **Mouvement Français Pour le Planning Familial** (4 sq. St-Irénée, 11e, tel. 01–48–07–29–10), part of the International Planned Parenthood Federation. You'll need a working knowledge of French to make much use of their services. **SOS Viol** (tel. 0–800–05–95–95) is a national rape crisis hotline; they'll answer calls weekdays 10–6.

Pacific Harbor Travel specializes in independent adventure travel with an emphasis on women's travel. They're one of the better known agencies for women's travel. *519 Seabright Ave., Suite 201, Santa Cruz, CA 95062, tel. 408/427-5000.*

Women Welcome Women (WWW) is a nonprofit organization aimed at bringing together women of all nationalities, ages, and interests. Membership can put you in touch with women around the globe. *Betty Sobel, U.S.A. Trustee, 10 Greenwood Lane, Westport, CT 06880, tel. 203/259-7832.*

RESOURCES FOR GAY AND LESBIAN TRAVELERS

The gay scene is alive and well in Paris, but lesbian spots are harder to find. Outside Paris, the gay scene is almost nonexistent, although a few cities and regions, particularly the Riviera, do have information centers and a bar or two. Fewer hate crimes are committed against gays in France than in the United States and the United Kingdom, but once you leave Paris, a less-than-warm welcome may await you in the more conservative provinces.

PUBLICATIONS *Are You Two . . . Together?* is the best known guide for lesbians traveling in Europe. It's fairly anecdotal and skimps on practical details like phone numbers and addresses, but it still makes an excellent read. It costs $18 and is published by Random House; ask for it at your local bookstore.

Spartacus bills itself as *the* guide for the gay traveler, with practical tips and reviews of hotels and agencies in more than 160 countries. It's a bit expensive at $32.95, though you do get snappy color photos and listings in four languages. *Box 422458, San Francisco, CA 94142, tel. 800/462-6654.*

One of the better gay and lesbian travel newsletters is *Out and About,* with listings of gay-friendly hotels and travel agencies, plus health cautions for travelers with HIV. A 10-issue subscription costs $49; single issues cost about $5. *Tel. 800/929-2268 for subscriptions.*

The most comprehensive lesbian publication is **Women's Traveller** ($11.95), a dense guide to bars, hotels, and agencies throughout the United States, Canada, and the Caribbean. Rumor has it that a European edition will debut soon; keep your eyes open. *Box 422458, San Francisco, CA 94142, tel. 415/255–0404 or 800/462–6654.*

ORGANIZATIONS International Gay Travel Association (IGTA) is a nonprofit organization with worldwide listings of travel agencies, gay-friendly hotels, gay bars, and travel services. *Box 4974, Key West, FL 33041, tel. 800/448–8550, fax 305/286–6633.*

International Lesbian and Gay Association (ILGA) is an excellent source for info about conditions, specific resources, and trouble spots in dozens of countries, including France. *81 rue Marche au Charbon, 1000 Brussels 1, Belgium, tel. 02/502–24–71.*

TRAVELERS WITH DISABILITIES

Accessibility may soon have an international symbol if an initiative begun by the Society for the Advancement of Travel for the Handicapped (SATH) catches on. A bold, underlined, capital *H* is the symbol that SATH is publicizing for hotels, restaurants, and tourist attractions to indicate that the property has some accessible facilities. While awareness of the needs of travelers with disabilities increases every year, budget opportunities are harder to find. Always ask if discounts are available, either for you or for a companion. In addition, plan your trip and make reservations far in advance, since companies that provide services for people with disabilities go in and out of business regularly.

The government has published an excellent, free booklet (in French), "Touristes Quand Même." It details, region by region, which transportation systems and tourist attractions are accessible to the disabled. The booklet is available from tourist offices and from Paris's **Comité National Français de Liaison pour la Réadaptation des Handicapés** (236 bis rue de Tolbiac, 13e, tel. 01–53–80–66–66).

ACCOMMODATIONS Whenever possible, reviews in this book will indicate if rooms are wheelchair accessible. Many hotels, however, are in buildings that are hundreds of years old and unsuited to guests with impaired mobility. In general, more expensive or chain hotels are better equipped. Talk to the **Association des Paralysés de France** (17 blvd. Auguste-Blanqui, 13e, tel. 01–40–78–69–00) for a list of wheelchair-accessible hotels.

GETTING AROUND Most major airlines are happy to help travelers with disabilities make flight arrangements, provided they receive notification 48 hours in advance. Ask about possible discounts and check-in protocol when making reservations. The SNCF, France's rail service, has cars on some trains that are equipped for travelers with disabilities and passengers in wheelchairs can be escorted on and off trains. All places for those in wheelchairs are now in no-smoking cars. Contact SNCF in Paris (tel. 08–36–35–35–35) to request this service in advance and for tickets; for more wheelchair-access information, try the **SNCF Accessibilité Service** (toll-free in France, tel. 0–800–15–47–53). Most trains and train stations in Western Europe are wheelchair accessible, though some in more remote locations are not.

PUBLICATIONS Twin Peaks Press publishes *Travel for the Disabled,* which offers helpful hints as well as a comprehensive list of guidebooks and facilities geared to disabled travelers. Their *Directory of Travel Agencies for the Disabled* lists more than 350 agencies throughout the world. Each is $19.95 plus $3 shipping and handling ($4.50 for both). Twin Peaks also offers a "Traveling Nurse's Network," which connects travelers with registered nurses to aid and accompany them on their trip. Travelers fill out an application that Twin Peaks matches to nurses' applications in their files. Fees range from $30 to $125. *Box 129, Vancouver, WA 98666, tel. 360/694–2462 or 800/637–2256 for orders only.*

ORGANIZATIONS Directions Unlimited organizes individual and group tours for disabled travelers. *720 N. Bedford Rd., Bedford Hills, NY 10507, tel. 800/533–5343 or 914/241–1700 in NY.*

Flying Wheels Travel arranges cruises, tours, and vacation travel itineraries. *143 W. Bridge St., Box 382, Owatonna, MN 55060, tel. 800/535–6790 or 507/451–5005 in MN.*

Mobility International USA (MIUSA) is a nonprofit organization that coordinates exchange programs for disabled people around the world. MIUSA also offers information on accommodations and organized study programs for members ($25 annually). The French affiliate is **Comité National Français de Liaison pour la Réadaptation des Handicapés** (*see above*). Nonmembers may subscribe to the newsletter for $15. *Box 10767, Eugene, OR 97440, tel. and TDD 541/343–1284, fax 541/343–6812, miusa@igc.apc.org.*

Moss Rehabilitation Hospital's Travel Information Service provides information on tourist sights, transportation, accommodations, and accessibility in destinations around the world. You can request information by phone only. The service is free. *Tel. 215/456–9900, TDD 215/456–9602.*

WORKING IN FRANCE

If you're not currently a student (or recent grad), France won't grant you a work permit unless you already have a French employer who can convince immigration officials that he or she absolutely, positively needs *you*, and not a native French person, to fill the position. That said, plenty of native English speakers find work teaching their mother tongue to Francophones. Getting a decent teaching position isn't easy, but with some perseverance it is possible. Each of France's private English-language schools has its own guidelines and restrictions; many require a Teaching of English as a Foreign Language (TEFL) certificate, obtainable after an intensive four-week training course, and some hire only older, experienced teachers. The best place to get addresses and phone numbers is the Parisian *Pages jaunes* (Yellow Pages), and the best time to look is in late summer, since school generally starts around the beginning of October.

PUBLICATIONS *Studying and Working in France: A Student Guide* (St. Martin's; $17.95) offers help in applying for jobs in France, and it has info on university courses there. Council (*see* Budget Travel Organizations, *above*) publishes two excellent resource books with complete details on work/travel opportunities. The most valuable is **Work, Study, Travel Abroad: The Whole World Handbook** ($13.95), which gives the lowdown on scholarships, grants, fellowships, study-abroad programs, and work exchanges. Also worthwhile is Council's **The High-School Student's Guide to Study, Travel, and Adventure Abroad** ($13.95). Both books can be shipped to you book rate ($1.50) or first-class ($3).

The U.K.-based Vacation Work Press publishes two first-rate guides to working abroad: **Directory of Overseas Summer Jobs** ($14.95) and Susan Griffith's **Work Your Way Around the World** ($17.95). The first lists more than 45,000 jobs worldwide; the latter has fewer listings but makes a more interesting read. Look for them at bookstores, or you can contact the American distributor directly. *Peterson's: 202 Carnegie Center, Princeton, NJ 05843.*

ORGANIZATIONS **Au Pair Abroad** arranges board and lodging for people between the ages of 18 and 26 who want to work as nannies for three to 18 months in France. Basic language skills are required, and all applicants must go through a somewhat lengthy interview process. *1015 15th St. NW, Suite 750, Washington, D.C. 20005, tel. 202/408–5380, fax 202/480–5397, 708439@mcimail.com.*

The easiest way to arrange work in Britain, France, Ireland, and Germany is through Council's **Work Abroad Department** (205 E. 42nd St., New York, NY 10017, tel. 888/COUNCIL, http://www.ciee.org). The program enables you to work in Europe for three to six months. Participants must be U.S. citizens or permanent residents, 18 years or older, and a full-time student for the semester preceding their stay overseas. Past participants have worked at all types of jobs, including hotel and restaurant work, office and sales help, and occasionally career-related internships. A good working knowledge of French is required. The cost of the program is $200, which includes legal work-permission documents, orientation and program materials, access to job and housing listings, and ongoing support services overseas.

Canadians are not eligible for the Council Work Abroad program and should contact **Travel CUTS** (*see* Budget Travel Organizations, *above*), which has similar programs for Canadian students who want to work abroad for up to six months.

IAESTE sends full-time students abroad to practice their engineering, mathematics, and computer skills in more than 50 countries. You don't get pàid much, though the program is designed to cover day-to-day expenses. Applications are due between September and December for travel the following summer, so get going. *10 Corporate Center, Suite 250, 10400 Little Patuxent Pkwy., Columbia, MD 21044, tel. 410/997–2200, fax 410/997–5186.*

In Paris, **France USA Contacts (FUSAC)** has job listings for native English speakers with French-language ability. *3 rue Larochelle, 14e, tel. 01–45–38–56–57.*

STUDYING IN FRANCE

Studying in another country is the perfect way to scope out a foreign culture, meet locals, and improve your language skills. You may choose to study through a U.S.-sponsored program, usually through an American university, or to enroll in a program sponsored by a European organization. Do your homework; programs vary greatly in expense, academic quality, exposure to language, amount of contact with locals, and living conditions. Working through your local university is the easiest way to find out about study-abroad programs in France. Most universities have staff members that distribute information on programs at European universities, and they might be able to put you in touch with program participants.

The **American Institute for Foreign Study** and the **American Council of International Studies** arrange semester- and year-long study-abroad programs in universities throughout the world. Applicants must be enrolled as full- or part-time students. Fees vary according to the length of stay. *102 Greenwich Ave., Greenwich, CT 06830, tel. 800/727–2437.*

Council's **College and University Programs Division** administers summer-, semester-, and year-long study-abroad programs at various universities worldwide. To navigate the maze of programs, contact Council, or purchase their excellent *Work, Study, Travel Abroad: The Whole World Handbook* ($13.95).

The Information Center at the **Institute of International Education (IIE)** has reference books, foreign-university catalogues, study-abroad brochures, and other materials that may be consulted free of charge if you're in the neighborhood, or you can call for a recorded list of services. *809 U.N. Plaza, New York, NY 10017, tel. 212/984–5413. Information Center open Tues.–Thurs. 11–3:45.*

IIE also publishes the helpful *Academic Year Abroad* ($42.95), which lists more than 1,900 study-abroad programs for undergraduates and graduates. If you're more interested in summer-abroad and living-abroad programs, check out IIE's *Vacation Study Abroad* ($36.95). Order either from IIE Books (tel. 212/984–5412).

Coming and Going

CUSTOMS AND DUTIES

ARRIVING IN FRANCE Going through customs is usually pretty painless. The officials will check your passport but probably won't touch your luggage unless you look shady or their dogs have caught a whiff of something interesting in your bags. If you bring any foreign-made equipment with you from home, such as cameras or video gear, carry the original receipt or register it with customs before leaving the United States (ask for U.S. Customs Form 4457). Otherwise, you may end up paying duty on your return. Don't even *think* about drugs. Being cited for drug possession is no joke, and embassies and consulates often can't or won't do much to persuade officials to release you if you get tossed into prison. On top of that, immigration officials have been getting tougher, conducting random searches of any traveler they think looks remotely suspicious.

RETURNING HOME It's best to have all the souvenirs and gifts you're bringing home in an easily accessible place, just in case the officials would like to have a peek. Don't wrap your gifts—it makes customs officers very inquisitive.

➢ **U.S. CUSTOMS** • Like most government organizations, the U.S. Customs Service enforces a number of mysterious rules. When you return to the United States you have to declare all items you bought abroad, but you won't have to pay duty unless you come home with more than $400 worth of foreign goods, including items bought in duty-free stores. For purchases between $400 and $1,000 you have to pay a 10% duty. You also have to pay tax if you exceed your duty-free allowances: one liter of alcohol or wine (for those 21 and over), 100 non-Cuban cigars (sorry, Fidel) or 200 cigarettes, and one bottle of perfume. A free leaflet about customs regulations and illegal souvenirs, "Know Before You Go," is available from the **U.S. Customs Service** (Box 7407, Washington, D.C. 20044, tel. 202/927–6724).

➢ **CANADIAN CUSTOMS** • Exemptions for returning Canadians range from $20 to $500, depending on how long you've been out of the country: For two days out, you're allowed to return with C$200 worth of goods; for one week out, you're allowed C$500 worth. Above these limits, you'll be taxed about 15%. Duty-free limits are: up to 50 cigars, 200 cigarettes, 400 grams of tobacco, and 1.14 liters of liquor—all must be declared in writing upon arrival at customs and must be with you or in your checked baggage. To mail back gifts, label the package: "Unsolicited Gift—Value under C$60." For more scintillating details, call the automated information line of the **Revenue Canada Customs, Excise and Taxation Department** (2265 St. Laurent Blvd. S., Ottawa, Ont. K1G 4K3, tel. 613/993–0534 or 613/991–3881), where you may request a copy of the Canadian Customs brochure "I Declare/Je Déclare."

➢ **U.K. CUSTOMS** • Travelers age 17 or over who return to the United Kingdom may bring back the following duty-free goods: 200 cigarettes or 100 cigarillos or 50 cigars or 250 grams of tobacco; 1 liter of alcohol over 22% volume or 2 liters of alcohol under 22% volume, plus 2 liters of still table wine; 60 ml of perfume and 250 ml of toilet water; and other goods worth up to £136. If returning from another EU country, you can choose, instead, to bring in the following, provided they were *not* bought in a duty-free shop: 300 cigarettes or 150 cigarillos or 75 cigars or 400 grams of tobacco; 1.5 liters of alcohol over 22% volume or three liters of alcohol under 22% volume, plus 5 liters of still table wine; 75 grams of perfume and ⅜ liter of toilet water; and other goods worth up to £250. For further information or a copy of "A Guide for Travellers," which details standard customs procedures as well as what you may bring into the United Kingdom from abroad, contact **HM Customs and Excise** (Dorset House, Stamford St., London SE1 9PY, tel. 0171/928–3344).

➢ **AUSTRALIAN CUSTOMS** • Australian travelers 18 and over may bring back, duty free: 1 liter of alcohol; 250 grams of tobacco products (equivalent to 250 cigarettes or cigars); and other articles worth up to AUS$400. If you're under 18, your duty-free allowance is AUS$200. To avoid paying duty on goods you mail back to Australia, mark the package: "Australian goods returned." For more rules and regulations, request the pamphlet "Customs Information for Travellers" from a local **Collector of Customs** (GPO Box 8, Sydney NSW 2001, tel. 02/226–5997).

➢ **NEW ZEALAND CUSTOMS** • Travelers over age 17 are allowed, duty-free: 200 cigarettes or 250 grams of tobacco or 50 cigars or a combo of all three up to 250 grams; 4.5 liters of wine or beer and one 1,125-ml bottle of spirits; and goods with a combined value up to NZ$700. If you want more details, ask for the pamphlet "Customs Guide for Travellers" from a New Zealand consulate.

BY AIR

If you can't get a cheap flight into Paris, look into other destinations. Flying into Brussels is convenient; the train trip to Paris costs about 250F second class, takes about three hours, and the train station connects to the airport in Brussels. Amsterdam and Frankfurt are also good bets. One-way second-class train tickets cost 390F and 550F respectively. On your fateful departure day, remember that check-in time for international flights is two hours before departure. One more thing: Many international flights lasting more than six hours allow smoking—so if fumes make you queasy, book short hops or ask for seats as far away from the smoking section as possible; if you love to light up, book long and straight.

FROM NORTH AMERICA The flight from the East Coast to Paris takes about eight hours; from the West Coast, you're looking at 12. Plenty of U.S. airlines, including **American** (tel. 800/433–7300), **Continental** (tel. 800/231–0856), **Delta** (tel. 800/221–1212), **TWA** (tel. 800/892–4141), and **United** (tel. 800/241–6522) fly from all over the United States to Paris. **Air France** (tel. 800/237–2747) has frequent flights to Paris and other French cities. Call around to see who is offering the best fare at the moment. With a little advance planning and flexibility, you should be able to get a ticket for about $600 almost any time of year.

Air Canada (tel. 800/361–8620 in Québec or 800/268–7240 in Ontario) flies to Paris direct from Montréal, Toronto, and sometimes Vancouver. **Canadian Airlines** (tel. 800/426–7000) has lots of flights from Toronto.

FROM THE U.K. Air France (tel. 0181/759–2311) and **British Airways** (tel. 0181/897–4000) make the hour flight from London's Gatwick and Heathrow airports to Paris several times a day. The cost of a round-trip ticket is almost halved if you purchase it 14 days in advance and stay over a Saturday night. Both airlines also fly to Paris a few times every day from London's most central airport, London City. **Nouvelles Frontières** (tel. 0171/629–7772) in London has info on discounted airfares between the two countries.

FROM DOWN UNDER Qantas (tel. 02/957–0111) can get you to Paris from Sydney by way of Frankfurt. **Continental** (tel. 02/693–5266 in Sydney or 09/379–5682 in Auckland) flies to Paris from Melbourne, Sydney, and Auckland, New Zealand, by way of Los Angeles and New York. Round-trip fares go as low as AUS$2,000 but are often as high as AUS$6,000. Talk to the STA offices in Victoria or Auckland (*see* Budget Travel Organizations, *above*) for info on discount fares.

TAKING LUGGAGE ABROAD You've heard it a million times. Now you'll hear it again: Pack light. U.S. airlines allow passengers to check two pieces of luggage, neither of which can exceed 62 linear inches (length + width + height) or weigh more than 70 pounds. If your airline accepts excess baggage, it will probably charge you for it. Foreign airline policies vary, so call or check with a travel agent before you show up at the airport with one bag too many.

If you're traveling with a pack, tie all loose straps to each other or onto the pack itself, as they tend to get caught in luggage conveyer belts. Put valuables like cameras and important documents in the middle of packs, wadded inside clothing, because outside pockets are vulnerable to probing fingers.

Anything you'll need during the flight (and valuables to be kept under close surveillance) should be stowed in a carry-on bag. Foreign airlines have different policies but generally allow only one carry-on in tourist class, in addition to a handbag and a bag filled with duty-free goodies. The carry-on bag cannot exceed 45 inches (length + width + height) and must fit under the seat or in the overhead luggage compartment. Call for the airline's current policy. Passengers on U.S. airlines are limited to one carry-on bag, plus coat, camera, and handbag. Carry-on bags must fit under the seat in front of you; maximum dimensions are 9 x 45 x 22 inches. Hanging bags can have a maximum dimension of 4 x 23 x 45 inches; to fit in an overhead bin, bags can have a maximum dimension of 10 x 14 x 36 inches. If your bag is too porky for compartments, be prepared for the humiliation of rejection and last-minute baggage check.

BY EUROTUNNEL

Since the early 1800s, visionaries had dreamed of building a tunnel between France and England, but endless obstacles stood in the way. The Channel itself wasn't a problem—the chalk on the Channel floor is actually quite firm and amenable to tunneling—but bureaucratic fumbling and money problems delayed the opening of the tunnel considerably. Yet despite this nearly two-century delay, the Eurotunnel is now complete, and it offers Parisians and Londoners daily opportunities for cultural exchange. **Eurostar** (19 Worple Rd., Wimbledon, tel. 0181/784–1333) sells second-class tickets for the train trip from London to Paris for 645F one-way (395F if bought 15 days in advance). The trip takes three hours. If you're traveling by car, **Le Shuttle** (19 rue des Mathurins, 9e, Paris, tel. 01–47–42–50–00) sells round-trip tickets from Calais to Folkestone for 350F and up. However, Le Shuttle prices fluctuate

Ferry companies are working hard to undercut the Eurotunnel, and P&O Ferries occasionally offers round trips for 20F a passenger. The catch is that you have to complete your trip within 48 hours—but how they force you to use the return portion of your ticket is unclear.

depending on time of day, the week you travel in, and the length of your stay, so be sure to check prices before making any plans. The trip takes about 40 minutes.

BY FERRY

Lots of ferry and Hovercraft companies transport travelers and their cars across the Channel, and with the arrival of the Euro-tunnel, many ferry companies are slashing their prices. Calais is becoming the Channel-crossing hub; only **Hoverspeed** (tel. 03–21–46–14–14) still sends speedy Seacats between Boulogne and Folkestone (mid-April–September only). From Calais, **Sealink** (tel. 01–44–94–40–40) and **P&O Ferries** (tel. 01–44–51–00–51) make the 1½-hour ferry trip to Dover all year long for 200F round trip if you stay fewer than five days, 400F round-trip if you stay more. Hoverspeed sends Hovercrafts over in half the time and charges 200F round-trip for stays of fewer than five days.

Staying in France

GETTING AROUND

BY TRAIN The railway system in France is fast, extensive, and efficient. All French trains have a first and second class. First class is 30%–50% more expensive, though the difference in comfort between the two is minimal, except on the lightning-fast TGV trains, on which first class is really deluxe. First-class sleeping cars are very expensive, but second-class *couchettes*, bunks that come six to a compartment, cost only 90F more (and are worth every centime). On some international trips, you may be forced to pay a hefty supplement for a nice bed, whether you want to or not; check in advance to make sure you can get a 90F couchette. For long distances, it's best to take the TGV trains, though a seat reservation (which runs 20F–90F) is required *without exception* on these trains. For info on the various passes and discount tickets available, *see* Rail Passes, *above*. To make reservations on any train in France, call 08–36–35–35–35, or stop by the local train station.

Purchase your ticket at the booth in the station before boarding the train. And don't forget to validate it (*composter le billet*) at the orange ticket puncher, usually located at the entrance to the *quai* (platform). That said, if you board your train on the run and don't have time to punch it, look for a *contrôleur* as soon as possible and get him to sign it. Otherwise, you're in for a nasty *amende* (fine). Train schedules for individual lines are available at all stations through which the line runs. Complete SNCF timetables are available at info counters in large stations. It's a good idea to bring food and drink with you on long trips; the food sold on the train is usually very expensive and very bad.

BY BUS Buses, slightly less expensive and significantly slower than the trains, are generally used only to fill in the gaps left by the rail lines. You buy tickets for short distances when boarding. For greater distances, buy the tickets in advance at the bus station. Buses are generally clean, comfortable, and punctual. **Gare Internationale Eurolines** in Paris (28 av. du Général de Gaulle, tel. 01–49–72–51–51) offers international service to many European cities, including London (9 hrs, 410F round-trip), Berlin (12 hrs, 750F round-trip), and Barcelona (15 hrs, 880F round-trip).

BY CAR Having a car gives you the ultimate travel freedom. Gas, however, is expensive in France (about 5F80 per liter). Remember while driving in France that drivers on your right, even if they are coming from a minor road, have the right of way—and they will take it. If you plan to rent a car abroad, you should probably get an International Driver's Permit (IDP) before leaving home. The IDP is available from the American Automobile Association (AAA) for $16; if you bring two passport photos, the cost is only $10 (non–AAA members will pay a few dollars more). Some offices can take photos for you, and nonmembers must pay cash. Some offices can issue an IDP on the spot in about 15 minutes, but be sure to call ahead; during the busy season IDPs can take a week or more.

The French motoring club **Automobile Club National (ACN)** (5 rue Auber, 75009 Paris, tel. 01–44–51–53–99, fax 01–49–24–93–99) charges a small fee for towing (tel. 0–800–05–05–01) and roadside breakdown service. If you're a AAA member, you can get reimbursed for ACN charges when you get home. For more info stop by your local AAA branch and ask for the pamphlet "Offices to Serve You Abroad." Or send a S.A.S.E. to the AAA's head office (1000 AAA Drive, Heathrow, FL 32746).

➣ **RENTING A CAR** • Although renting a car is more expensive in France than in the United States, several agencies offer pretty reasonable rates that are worth it if several people split the cost. Tiny stick shifts go for around 300F per day or 1,000F–1,500F for a week, and some agencies include mileage, while others may charge extra. Many agencies require that you be at least 23 years old and have a credit card. Major car rental companies include **Renault Eurodrive** (650 First Ave., New York, NY 10016, tel. 800/221–1052), **Auto Europe** (Box 7006, Portland, ME 04112, tel. 207/828–2525 or 800/223–5555), **Avis** (in Paris, tel. 01–45–50–32–31), and **Budget Rent-a-Car** (3350 Boyington St., Carrollton, TX 75006, tel. 800/527–0700; in Paris, tel. 01–46–86–65–65), and **Europe by Car** (1 Rockefeller Plaza, New York, NY 10020, tel. 800/223–1516). Airports and large train stations have rental agencies on site.

You can save as much as 30% if you reserve a car before leaving home, rather than renting one on the spot abroad.

BY MOTORBIKE/MOPED Any two-wheeled vehicle that goes over 50 kilometers (31 miles) per hour needs to be registered and licensed at the *préfecture* (police headquarters). This means most mopeds don't have to be registered and most motorbikes do. Renting a moped is expensive (about 150F to 300F per day), but may be worth doing to really get off the beaten track for a day or two.

BY BIKE French roads are well suited for bicycling. Michelin road maps distinguish major roads (marked in red) from minor ones (yellow) and local routes (white). You can pay anywhere from about 60F to 120F to rent a bike for a day; a VTT (*vélo tout terrain*, or mountain bike) is generally more expensive than your average three-speed. Train stations often have rental agencies. The **Fédération Française de Cyclotourisme** (8 rue Jean-Marie-Jégo, 13e, Paris, tel. 01–45–80–30–21) can provide you with more information about biking in France.

Transporting your bicycle from one place to another shouldn't be too difficult. On most local trains in France, you can bring your bicycle aboard for free. On others—generally those that cross regional or international borders—you have to register your bike as luggage (150F). The publication "Guide du Train et Vélo," available at large train stations, provides complete information on the train and bicycle combination.

HITCHING Hitchhike at your own risk. Hitching is not uncommonly dangerous in France, but psychos and reckless drivers come in every nationality. To maximize your chances of getting a lift, look neat, carry a minimal amount of luggage, and hold a sign telling passersby where you want to go. In regions where American travelers are scarce (like the north), displaying a U.S. flag over your pack might help you get a ride; elsewhere, this strategy could leave you stranded for days. For organized (and expensive) hitching, contact **Allo Stop,** an organization that links up hitchers and drivers for a membership fee (about 250F for two years, or 30F–70F each time, depending on the distance) plus 20 centimes per kilometer to the driver. Contact their main office in Paris (tel. 01–53–20–42–42) for information and locations of branch Allo Stop offices.

BUSINESS HOURS

Most museums are closed one day a week (often Tuesday) and on national holidays (*see* National Holidays, *above*). Normal opening times are from 9:30 to 5 or 6, often with a long lunch break between noon and 2. Many are open afternoons only on Sundays. Large stores stay open from 9 or 9:30 in the morning until 6 or 7 in the evening, without a lunch break. Smaller shops often open an hour or so earlier and close a few hours later, but with a lengthy lunch

More
To see the real
France
Insider's France
for less
Take to the roads
money.

347 AGA 92

EURODRIVE BENEFITS INCLUDE:

- Low, tax-free rates for trips from 17 days to 6 months
- Full insurance coverage good in 27 countries
- Minimum age of only 18 years
- Wide range of brand-new, fuel-efficient cars
- Free pickups and returns throughout France
- Unlimited mileage   • 24-hour roadside service
- Thousands of satisfied customers

To save money with the insider's car plan, call Eurodrive.

Our *low, tax-free rates* on comfortable, brand-new cars are truly all-inclusive and can save you hundreds of dollars off rental car costs.

RENAULT EURODRIVE

l'Europe en Liberté
The Alternative to Car Rental

Call 1-800-221-1052

From Western states, call 1-800-477-7116
650 First Avenue,
New York, NY 10016

Travel Agent inquiries welcome

BER97FR

break in between. Banks are open weekdays (and sometimes Saturdays) roughly 9:30 in the morning to 4:30 in the afternoon. Most banks take a one-hour or 90-minute lunch break.

EMERGENCIES

In an emergency, dial 17 for the **police,** 15 for an **ambulance,** and 18 for the **fire department.** If you run into trouble on the streets, the best thing to do is yell for help *(au secours!)* and attract as much attention as possible. In case you lose your French with your cool, here are a few phrases to keep you going: *urgence* (emergency), *samu* (ambulance), *pompiers* (firemen), *poste de police* (police station), *docteur* (doctor), and *hôpital* (hospital).

For nonemergency situations, look in the phone directory for the number of the *commissariat* or *gendarmerie,* both terms for the local police station; here you can report a theft or get the address of the local late-night pharmacies or pharmacist on call.

PHONES

Public phones are never far away in Paris; you will find them at post offices and often in cafés. On October 18, 1996, the French revamped their phone system and the old eight-digit phone number grew to 10 digits: All Paris numbers now start with 01, all numbers in the northwest start with 02, in the northeast 03, in the southeast 04, and in the southwest 05. If you come across an eight-digit number (now terribly passé), you have to know what part of France the number is in so you can tack on the new prefix. To make a call to France from another country, dial France's country code (33), drop the initial zero from the telephone number, and then dial the remaining nine digits.

LOCAL CALLS Local calls cost a minimum of 1F for six minutes. Most French phones only accept the **Télécarte,** a handy little card you can buy at tabacs, post offices, or Métro stations; it costs 41F for 50 units or 96F for 120 units. The digital display on the phone counts down your units while you're talking and tells you how many you have left when you hang up. The occasional old-fashioned phone will take 50-centime, 1F, 2F, and 5F coins, but it won't make change. Dial 12 with a card or coin to reach directory inquiries from any phone (though operators rarely speak English).

INTERNATIONAL CALLS To dial direct to another country, dial 19 + the country code (61 for Australia, 64 for New Zealand, 44 for the United Kingdom, and 1 for the United States and Canada) plus the area code and number. The cheapest time to call is between 10:30 PM and 6 AM (about 6F40 per minute to the U.S. and 4F per minute to the U.K.). Middling rates apply between 6 AM and 8 AM and 9:30 PM and 10:30 PM, and Sundays and holidays have reduced rates all day long. Calling anywhere over 100 kilometers (62 miles) from France in the middle of a weekday will run you around 3F20 per minute. The Télécarte (*see* Local Calls, *above*) will come in handy for making any of these long-distance calls, though you may have five minutes or less of quality time with mom and dad before you're cut off. To use an **AT&T** calling card or to talk to their international operators, dial 0–800–99–00–11. For **MCI,** dial 0–800–99–00–19; for **Sprint,** dial 0–800–99–00–87. Within France, you can call collect by dialing 12 for the operator and saying *"en PCV"* ("on pay say vay").

MINITEL In 1990, France Telecom proudly launched the distribution of an information device called the Minitel: a monitor/modem that can receive electronic mail, conduct data searches, dole out addresses and telephone numbers, and even tell you the weather. You can use them for free in any post office, where Minitel terminals have for the most part replaced telephone books. Here's how it works: Press the button with a phone-receiver symbol on it and dial "11." When you hear the high-pitched tone, press ANNIHILATION. Database fields will then appear on the screen. Type in the *nom* (name), *activité* (subject), *localité* (city), or address relating to the info you're seeking. To advance a line press SUITE, to go back a line press RETOUR, to backspace press CORRECTION, and to begin a new search press ANNIHILATION. Press ENVOI to send your query; responses will then appear on the screen. To end your session, press CONNEXION/FIN.

MAIL

Airmail letters and postcards to the United States and Canada cost 4F50 for 20 grams. Letters to the United Kingdom cost 3F. Postcards sent to most European countries cost 2F80, 5F10 to Australia and New Zealand. Buy stamps (*timbres*) in post offices if you really like standing in line. Otherwise, buy them at one of the ubiquitous tabacs. You can identify post offices by the yellow signs with blue letters that say LA POSTE; mailboxes are yellow, with one slot for letters heading for places within the region of France you're in, and one for *autres destinations* (everywhere else).

RECEIVING MAIL American Express will hold mail gratis for cardholders, 2F–10F per piece for the rest of the world. Local post offices also hold mail that is marked POSTE RESTANTE. Have your pen pals address your letter with your last name first, in capital letters, and make sure they include the postal code.

WHERE TO SLEEP

HOTELS Hotels in France are classified by the state in categories ranging from no stars to four stars. A room with a *douche* (shower) is always cheaper than one with a *baignoire* (bath), but the cheapest rooms often have just a sink and sometimes a bidet. The toilet is usually down the hall. Ask for *le prix le plus bas* (the lowest price) and you'll be shown to the rooms with the least plumbing. You'll save lots of money by doing without your own private bath, but expect to pay about 15F–25F for a shower down the hall. Prices must, by law, be posted at the hotel entrance, but they don't always match the price the proprietor asks. Hotel tax usually runs 2F per person per night and usually is not included in the posted price. *Petit déjeuner* (breakfast) is offered in most places but costs about 20F–30F—a high price for a piece of baguette and coffee. Hotels fill up quickly in the summer, and it's a good idea to reserve ahead.

Just so you know, the price categories used in this book always refer to the cost of a double room plus tax.

CHAMBRES D'HOTE *Chambres d'hôte* (bed-and-breakfasts), popular in rural areas, can be relatively cheap, but don't expect to wake in a charming seaside cottage to a breakfast with homemade jam; the French version of the bed-and-breakfast is more often just a spare room that a local family rents out. Check with the local tourist office for the scoop.

HOSTELS Although cheap hotel accommodations in France are easy to find, there's nothing like a youth hostel for meeting other travelers—something about sharing squeaky bunk beds and cold showers really seems to bring people together. Sometimes there isn't much economic reason for staying in a hostel, though, since they're often far out of town and you end up spending as much for transportation as you're saving by staying there.

Most hostels in France are run by **FUAJ** (Fédération Unie des Auberges de Jeunesse), which puts out a great pamphlet showing the location of all the hostels with their addresses, phone numbers, and details like price and accessibility to hiking. Get the pamphlet at an HI office before you leave home, or ask for it at any French hostel. Most hostels run between 50F and 100F per night, and many include breakfast.

GITES D'ETAPE Another cheap alternative, especially in rural areas (e.g., the Alps, the Vercors), is the *gîte d'étape* (rural hostel). Like hostels, gîtes usually feature dorm rooms and community showers and are occasionally housed in fantastic rustic buildings. Although they're often technically reserved for hikers, budget travelers can usually wheedle their way in. Some gîtes cost as little as 30F a night, others up to 50F. The **Fédération Nationale des Gîtes de France** (59 rue St-Lazare, 9e, Paris, tel. 01–49–70–75–75) has a book of gîtes with prices, capacity, and photos of rentals all around France.

UNIVERSITY AND STUDENT HOUSING As soon as students go home for the summer, many French schools rent out their rooms to travelers. To get a spot in one of these student dorms, contact the local **Centre Régional des Œuvres Universitaires (CROUS)**. See the Where to Sleep section in individual cities for local CROUS telephone numbers.

APARTMENT STAYS For groups of people staying in one place for more than a week, renting an apartment is an enticing option. In summer, especially, it's pretty easy to find a place for 1,000F–2,000F per month; owners will often work out a weekly deal if they're desperate. The *France USA Contacts* newspaper, available around Paris (try Shakespeare and Co. bookstore on the quay across from Notre-Dame), has a bunch of listings, as do CRIJ (Centre Régional Information Jeunesse) offices in larger cities.

CAMPING Camping in much of France is not for those who seek peaceful seclusion among trees and streams; it's more for those who like nestling up to a family-filled caravan in a shady parking lot on the outskirts of town. Unless you have some backwoods adventures in mind and plan to be far from the big cities in regions like the Alps or Brittany, it may not be worth schlepping your camping gear to France. Campgrounds usually charge anywhere from 30F to 80F per person depending on the facilities. Local tourist offices have lists of nearby campgrounds, all of which are marked by a little caravan sign.

FOOD

It's not by chance that France is known as one of the culinary capitals of the world; food is as important to French culture as the language. Whether it's a 15F crêpe from a sidewalk stand at 2 AM or a 90F menu at the traditional 8 PM dinner hour, the food you eat in France will make you rethink returning to the burgers and fries or fish-and-chips from whence you came.

Supermarkets are plentiful and offer the best prices for your basics, but small *boucheries* (butcher shops) and *fromageries* (cheese shops) will sell you meats and cheeses by the slice for about the same price. *Charcuteries* are generally delis that offer fresh salads and take-out stuff like quiche or lasagna that is sold by weight for pretty good prices. *Boulangeries* sell bread, and sometimes pastries, while *pâtisseries* sell pastries almost exclusively. Beware of small corner stores that often charge twice as much as big chain stores like Casino, Super U, Prisunic, and Monoprix.

It would be a crime, though, not to eat in a restaurant at least once in a while in France. Many restaurants offer a *plat du jour,* which includes meat, veggies, and pasta or potatoes, for around 50F. If you're hungry, your best bet is to order a *prix fixe menu,* which will include at least three courses for 60F–120F, instead of ordering from the *carte* (menu). Try to eat your big meal in the middle of the day, when prices are often reduced by about a third. Restaurants operate in two shifts: Lunch is served from noon to 2:30 and dinner 7–10. Restaurants don't get full until around 8 PM. Eating out is usually an elaborate affair; a three-course meal is the norm. To avoid paying 15F for bottled water, which the waiter will inevitably try to serve, order simply a "carafe d'eau" (a carafe of tap water).

Cafés, generally open all day and often late into the evening, usually offer croissants and other pastries and sometimes more substantial fare like baguettes topped with cheese or meat. Coffee and croissants or *tartines* (baguettes spread with butter) are the French version of breakfast. Brasseries serve up standard meals like *steak-frites* (steak with french fries) or roast chicken for 50F or so. In major cities, McDonald's and Quick rear their ugly heads. Yet the best fast-food deal is the good ol' 25F *donner-kebabs* (gyros) that can be found in most large towns. Crêpe stands also sell quick fixes for 12F–25F.

PARIS AND THE ILE-DE-FRANCE

2

By Viviana Mahieux and Julia Švihra

To understand what Paris is all about, you need to understand the city's brooms. Over a decade ago, Paris decided to remake itself as the cleanest metropolis in the world. The city didn't want American-style urban renewal (this was tried unsuccessfully in the '60s and '70s), nor did it want to turn deteriorated neighborhoods into cutesy historical districts (that's Disney's domain). The idea was to keep Paris looking the same—only cleaner—so some bureaucrat decided to institute the regular sweeping of every street in Paris by hand. Of course, to do this they needed the perfect broom. After a painstaking search for the most efficient street-cleaning broom, a committee of urban undersecretaries settled on a traditional peasant model, like the ones made out of a bunch of twigs bound to a big stick. Of course, rather than use actual sticks and twigs, they came up with a durable plastic that could be cast in stick and twig molds. The plastic brooms look like their ancestors in almost every way—except for their fluorescent green color. Like the lime-green brooms used to sweep its streets, Paris is a strange concoction of tradition and high technology, of highly developed aesthetics and slightly screwy social conditions (observe the migrant workers pushing said peasant brooms).

Former president François Mitterrand was the man responsible for this project and other major changes in the Parisian landscape. His Grands Travaux (literally Big Projects, like the Pyramides du Louvre and La Défense) established him as one of the great builders in French history, along with Philippe August, Louis XIV, and Napoléon III. Even though the Grands Travaux are funded nationally, nearly all have been undertaken in Paris. Of course, this is no coincidence: To many, Paris *is* France. New president Jacques Chirac, however, is more intent on trimming the national budget than initiating new projects. The *fonctionnaire* (government worker) strikes that ripped through Paris in 1995 were a reaction to drastic cutbacks in social programs once taken for granted. If Chirac's shearing continues, the neon brooms and other urban renewal projects may someday elicit the same nostalgia as the original stick and twig ones they were based on.

Paradoxically, Paris is simultaneously a forum for politicians and self-appointed guardians of French tradition, as well as a magnet drawing poets, philosophers, and social butterflies. When the government outlawed the commercial use of non-French (i.e., English) words in 1993, an odd coalition of merchants, academics, and journalists came together to protest—and the law was soon ruled unconstitutional. And, while keepers of the cultural flame try to preserve all that they hold dear, they can't keep modernity from encroaching on this city, one of the great urban centers of Europe. These contradictory forces explain how the frumpiest, run-down neighborhood bistro will swipe your credit card through a hand-held computer, instantly debiting your account thousands of miles away for 1,000F of wine.

Paris's tension between tradition and modernity, though, is not always apparent as you walk down the street. The city usually seems as carefully orchestrated as ever: Students spiff up to see and be seen, and 85-year-old matrons do the shopping in smart little day suits—even Paris's parks, last bastions of nature, are planned down to the last blade of grass. But when you see a suited-up businessman *bavarder* (chatting) with an Algerian street-sweeper leaning on his broom in front of an Internet café, you'll suddenly realize that Paris is a city of sometimes startling contradictions.

Basics

AMERICAN EXPRESS At any of Paris's three AmEx travel offices, cardholders can pick up mail, buy traveler's checks in several currencies, and cash personal checks. The rue Scribe location is the most central and has several Métro lines running by it. Have your mail addressed to: your name, c/o American Express Voyages France, 11 rue Scribe, 75009 Paris. The office holds mail for 30 days. Non-cardholders can also receive mail (though it costs 5F for each pickup) and buy traveler's checks with French francs. Everyone can use the travel agencies and currency exchange offices. *11 rue Scribe, 9e, tel. 01–47–77–79–50. Métro: Opéra. Open weekdays 9–6:30, Sat. 9–5:30. Other locations: 38 av. de Wagram, 8e, tel. 01–42–27–58–80; Métro: Ternes; open weekdays 9–5:30. 5 rue de Chaillot, 16e, tel. 01–47–23–72–15; Métro: Iéna; open weekdays 9–5.*

BUREAUX DE CHANGE During business hours (9 or 10 AM–5 or 6 PM) you can get good currency-exchange rates around the Opéra Garnier, the Champs-Elysées, and the Palais Royal (rue de Rivoli); just be sure you stop in at an official bank and not one of the bureaux de change, which keep longer hours but get away with worse rates. The bureaux at the train stations stay open until at least 8 PM, sometimes as late as 10 PM. There are other bureaux near the Champs Elysées and in the Quartier Latin around the intersection of boulevards St-Germain and St-Michel. There are a few others scattered on the rue de Rivoli close to the Métro Hotel de Ville. Rates are generally worse on the Left Bank than on the Right.

In theory, the best way to change money is to use an ATM machine; you get francs at the excellent commercial exchange rate, and the transaction fees may be lower than the interest charged by your credit card for cash withdrawals. Trouble is, the machines are very picky and temperamental, so your card may only work sporadically; make sure you have a backup method of getting money. When your card does work, withdraw as much as you think safe to carry. The ubiquitous **BNP** (Banque National de Paris) machines will accept cards on both Cirrus and Star systems—give 'em a go when you pass by. The most reliable Cirrus ATMs are housed at **Crédit Mutuel** banks; try 8 rue Saint Antoine, 4e (Métro: St-Paul); 2 rue de l'Arrivée, 15e (Métro: Montparnasse-Bienvenue); or 13 rue des Abbesses, 18e (Métro: Abbesses). Plus-system cardholders should try **Bred** banks with Right Bank–only locations, including 33 rue de Rivoli (Métro: Hôtel de Ville) and 14 boulevard des Capucines (Métro: Opéra).

For late-night currency exchange, you can use an automatic cash-exchange machine. To use exchange machines you need cash—and relatively crisp cash at that—and the exchange rate is not that great but, at 3 AM, who cares? Locations of 24-hour exchange machines include **Crédit du Nord** (24 blvd. Sébastopol, 1er); **CCF** (115 av. des Champs-Elysées, 8e); and **BNP** (2 pl. de l'Opéra, 2e).

DISCOUNT TRAVEL AGENCIES The following agencies can get you cheaper rates than most commercial travel agencies, as well as student identification cards (ISICs):

Access Voyages: *6 rue Pierre-Lescot, 1er, tel. 01–40–13–02–02. Métro: Rambuteau. Open weekdays 9–7, Sat. 10–6.* **Council Travel:** *6 rue de Vaugirard, 6e, tel. 01–46–34–02–90. Métro: Odéon. Open weekdays 9:30–6:30, Sat. 10–5. Other location: 22 rue des Pyramides, 1er, tel. 01–44–55–55–65. Métro: Pyramides.* **CPS Voyages (STA):** *20 rue des Carmes, 5e, tel. 01–43–25–00–76. Métro: Maubert-Mutualité.* **Forum Voyages:** *140 rue du Faubourg-St-Honoré, 8e, tel. 01–42–89–07–07. Métro: Champs-Elysées–Clemenceau. Open weekdays 9:30–7, Sat. 10–1 and 2–5.* **Usit Voyages:** *6 rue de Vaugirard, 6e, tel. 01–42–34–56–90. Métro: Odéon. Open weekdays 10–7, Sat. 1:30–5.*

Nouvelles Frontières. This is the place to go for discount airfares. *Central office: 63 blvd. des Batignolles, 8e, tel. 01–43–87–99–88. Métro: Villiers. Open Mon.–Sat. 9–7 (Thurs. until 8:30).*

Wasteels. This is the best-represented youth travel organization in town, with branches near most train stations. Here those under 26 can get 20% discounts on all train trips beginning or terminating in France. *113 blvd. St-Michel, 5e, tel. 01–43–26–25–25. RER: Luxembourg. Other location: 5 rue de la Banque, 2e, tel. 01–42–61–53–21. Métro: Bourse. Open weekdays 9–7.*

EMBASSIES **Australia.** *4 rue Jean-Rey, 15e, tel. 01–40–59–33–00, 01–40–59–33–01 in emergencies. Métro: Bir-Hakeim. Open weekdays 9–5:30.*

Canada. *35 av. Montaigne, 8e, tel. 01–44–43–29–16. Métro: Franklin D. Roosevelt. Open weekdays 8:30–11.*

Ireland. *4 rue Rude, 16e, tel. 01–45–00–20–87. Métro: Charles de Gaulle–Etoile. Open weekdays 9:30–noon.*

New Zealand. *7 ter rue Léonard-de-Vinci, 16e, tel. 01–45–00–24–11. Métro: Victor Hugo. Open weekdays 9–1 and 2–5:30.*

United Kingdom. *35 rue du Faubourg-St-Honoré, 8e, tel. 01–42–66–91–42. Métro: Madeleine. Open weekdays 9:30–1 and 2:30–6.*

United States. *2 rue St-Florentin, 1er, tel. 01–40–39–84–11 (in English) or 01–42–96–14–88 (in French). Métro: Concorde. Open weekdays 9–4.*

ENGLISH-LANGUAGE BOOKS AND NEWSPAPERS *The Free Voice,* a free monthly paper available at English-language bookstores, some restaurants, and the American Church (*see* Visitor Information, *below*), provides English-language commentary on Parisian life and lists upcoming events for the Anglophone community. English-language bookstores also carry the free *France USA Contacts,* which has classified listings in English and French for apartment rentals, goods for sale, work exchange, et cetera. Most newsstands carry the *International Herald-Tribune,* as well as international versions of *Time* and *Newsweek. Pariscope* (3F) has an English-language section called "Time Out," with recommendations for concerts, theater, movies, museum expositions, and even restaurant and bar picks. Their info can be slow on the update, so cross-check with the French-language listings. For more information on English-language bookstores in Paris, *see* Shopping, *below.*

LAUNDRY Make your mother happy and wash your jeans at a **Laverie Libre Service:** 9 rue de Jouy, 4e; 212 rue St-Jacques, 5e; 28 rue des Trois-Frères, 18e; 2 rue du Lappe, 11e; 28 rue Beaubourg, 3e; 113 rue Monge, 5e; 27 rue Vieille du Temple, 4e.

LOST AND FOUND **Service des Objets Trouvés.** The entire city shares one lost-and-found office, and this is it. They won't give info over the telephone; you have to trek over in person. *36 rue des Morillons, 15e, tel. 01–45–31–14–80. Métro: Convention. Open weekdays 8:30–5 (Tues. and Thurs. until 8).*

MAIL You can identify post offices by the yellow signs with blue letters that say LA POSTE. Mailboxes are yellow, with one slot for letters to Paris and one for AUTRES DESTINATIONS (everywhere else).

Hôtel des Postes. Paris's central post office is open 24 hours. At any time, day or night, the office offers mail, telephone, telegram, Minitel (*see* Phones, in Chapter 1), photocopy, and poste restante services. During regular business hours (weekdays 8–7, Saturday 8–noon) you can also use the fax machines and exchange money. All post offices in Paris accept poste restante mail, but this is where your mail will end up if the sender fails to specify a branch. Have your mail addressed to: LAST NAME, first name, Poste Restante, 75001 Paris. Bring your passport with you to pick it up. *52 rue du Louvre, at rue Etienne-Marcel, 1er, tel. 01–40–28–20–00. Métro: Sentier.*

The **post office** on the Champs-Elysées has extended hours for mail, telegram, and telephone service. *71 av. des Champs-Elysées, 8e, tel. 01–44–13–66–00. Métro: Franklin D. Roosevelt. Open Mon.–Sat. 8 AM–10 PM, Sun. 10–8.*

MEDICAL AID The **Hôpital Américain** (American Hospital), about a 45-minute trip outside Paris, operates a 24-hour emergency service. If you're American and lucky enough to have Blue Cross/Blue Shield (carry your card with you), they should cover the cost at the time of your visit.

On Wednesdays 1:30 PM–4:30 PM, anyone can walk into the Centre du Planning Familial (10 rue Vivienne, 2e, tel. 01–42–60–93–20; Métro: Bourse) for free info on contraception and STDs.

Otherwise, you have to pay up front and hope to be reimbursed by your insurance company when you return to the States. EU citizens also have to pay first but can be reimbursed while still in France if they have form E-111, available at some of the bigger post offices. *63 blvd. Victor-Hugo, Neuilly-sur-Seine, tel. 01–46–41–25–25. Take Métro to Pont de Neuilly, then follow blvd. du Château 15 min.*

Hôpital Anglais. The English Hospital, also known as the Hôpital Britannique, in Levallois, again about 45 minutes outside Paris, has 24-hour emergency service and two British doctors on duty. Here again, Americans have to pay up front and get reimbursed at home; EU citizens pay up front and can be reimbursed through form E-111. Most of the staff speaks no English. *3 rue Barbès, Levallois, tel. 01–46–39–22–22. Métro: Anatole-France.*

Centre de Soins MST. The Center for Sexually Transmitted Diseases provides free consultations on a drop-in basis, weekdays 5 PM–7 PM. You can sign in at 4:30. Although the staff speaks some English, flip through your French dictionary before you come in to prevent hazardous misunderstandings. *At Institut A. Fournier, 25 blvd. St-Jacques, 14e, tel. 01–40–78–26–00. Métro: St-Jacques.*

In a pinch, the American embassy (tel. 01–40–39–84–11) has a list of English-speaking doctors. Hotlines to **doctors** (tel. 01–47–07–77–77), **dentists** (SOS Dentaire, tel. 01–43–37–51–00), a **suicide hotline** (tel. 01–45–39–40–00), and a **poison center** (Centre Anti-Poison; tel. 01–40–37–04–04) are available for emergencies, but there's no guarantee the staff will speak English. For **AIDS** info, call 0–800–36–66–36; for **STD** info, call 01–40–78–26–00. Women who have been assaulted should call **SOS Femmes Battues** (14 rue Mendelssohn, 20e, tel. 01–43–48–20–40; Métro: Porte Montreuil). There are no doctors on call at English-speaking **SOS Help** (tel. 01–47–23–80–80), but between 3 PM and 11 PM they'll help you with medical referrals. For drug-related issues, **Drogues Info Service** (tel. 0–800–23–13–13) is a free 24-hour hotline. The staff speaks some English.

PHARMACIES Besides basic over-the-counter medication, pharmacies (identifiable by green neon crosses) provide all sorts of useful health and beauty aids. If you're looking for herbal (homeopathic) medicines, try the *pharmacies homéopathiques.*

While regular pharmacy hours are about 9 AM to 7 or 8 PM, **Pharmacie Dhéry** (84 av. des Champs-Elysées, 8e, tel. 01–45–62–02–41; Métro: George V) is open 24 hours. **Drugstore Publicis** (149 blvd. St-Germain, at rue de Rennes, 6e, tel. 01–42–22–92–50; Métro: St-Germain-des-Prés) is open daily until 2 AM. Three more pharmacies open until midnight are **Cariglioli** (10 blvd. Sépastopol, 4e, tel. 01–42–72–03–23; Métro: Châtelet); **La Nation** (13 pl. de la Nation, 11e, tel. 01–43–73–24–03; Métro: Nation); and **Caillaud** (6 blvd. des Capucines, 9e, tel. 01–42–65–88–29; Métro: Opéra).

VISITOR INFORMATION **Office de Tourisme de Paris.** Paris's main tourist office is an attraction in itself, with its gift shop, lodging desk, and multitude of glossy brochures—all a few seconds' walk from the Arc de Triomphe on the famed Champs-Elysées. The multilingual staff can give you info on public transport and other practicalities, and they're happy to tell you about current cultural events. The office sells *Télécartes* (phone cards), museum passes, and Paris Visite passes. Paris Visite passes are good for one, three, or five days of unlimited travel on Métro, bus, and RER lines; if you plan to hop on the Métro six or more times a day it *might* be worth it. If you're in a bind they can find lodging for you (8F–25F), but only if you come down to the office in person. They run out of brochures pretty regularly during peak tourist season, but try to secure **"Les Marchés de Paris,"** which lists all the markets in Paris, and **"Paris la nuit,"** which highlights nightclubs and late-night restaurants. Both are free and in French. For 24-hour info in English on upcoming art exhibits and festivals, dial the cultural hotline at 01–49–52–53–56. *127 av. des Champs-Elysées, 8e, tel. 01–49–52–53–54. Métro: Charles de Gaulle–Etoile. Open daily 9–8.*

Six branch offices also reserve rooms and dole out info on the city. The one at the **Eiffel Tower** (7e, tel. 01–45–51–22–15) is open May through September only, 11–6. Other branch offices in the main train stations are open 8–8 most of the year and until 9 in summer (though Austerlitz closes at 3 PM): **Gare d'Austerlitz** (13e, tel. 01–45–84–91–70); **Gare de l'Est** (10e, tel. 01–46–07–17–73); **Gare de Lyon** (12e, tel. 01–43–43–33–24); **Gare Montparnasse** (15e, tel. 01–43–22–19–19); and **Gare du Nord** (10e, tel. 01–45–26–94–82). All of them are closed on Sunday.

The **Accueil des Jeunes en France** (Reception Center for Young People in France) is more in tune with the backpack set. The folks that staff AJF's four offices book rooms in hostels for a 10F fee and sell ISIC cards (*see* Planning Your Trip, Student ID Cards, in Chapter 1) for 60F. The AJF also acts as a travel agency for many budget-travel packages—a great way to have someone organize your trip for you and to meet some mellow people. To avoid the huge crowds during the summer tourist rush, arrive right after it opens at 9 AM. *119 rue St-Martin, 4e, tel. 01–42–77–87–80. Métro: Rambuteau. Open Mon.–Sat. 9–5:45. Other locations: Gare du Nord, 10e, tel. 01–42–85–86–19; Métro: Gare du Nord; open summer, daily 8 AM–10 PM. 139 blvd. St-Michel, 5e, tel. 01–43–54–95–86; RER: Port Royal; open Mar.–Oct., Mon.–Sat. 10–6.*

The utterly helpful **Eglise Américaine** (American Church) hosts concerts and holiday meals and lists jobs, apartments, and contacts for expatriates. It's a great place to meet other Americans staying in the city. *65 quai d'Orsay, 7e, tel. 01–47–05–07–99. Métro: Invalides. Open Mon.–Sat. 9 AM–10:30 PM, Sun. 2 PM–7:30 PM.*

COMING AND GOING

BY PLANE Paris's main airports lie a fair distance outside town—**Charles de Gaulle** (also called **Roissy**) is 26 kilometers (16 miles) to the northeast, **Orly** 16 kilometers (10 miles) to the south—but transportation to both is extensive. If you plan to fly out of Paris, arrive at the airport a full two hours before departure time; you'll probably encounter long lines at the ticket counters and baggage check and complete indifference from airline employees if you're about to miss your flight. Both airports have currency exchange desks and 24-hour cash exchange machines. *Airport info: Charles de Gaulle, tel. 01–48–62–22–80, 24 hours a day; Orly, tel. 01–49–75–15–15, daily 6 AM–11:30 PM.*

➤ **TO AND FROM THE AIRPORTS** • Both airports are served by **Air France buses** that depart for Paris every 12–15 minutes between 6 AM and 11 PM. The bus from Charles de Gaulle (55F) stops at the Air France office at Porte Maillot, not far from the Arc de Triomphe; the one from Orly (40F) runs to the Hôtel des Invalides. The trip takes about 40 minutes from Charles de Gaulle and 20 minutes from Orly, depending on traffic.

If you can afford a **taxi** from the airport, you've got more money than we do; it costs about 200F to get to the center of Paris from Charles de Gaulle and 160F from Orly. If you have a lot of stuff, you might want to take the Air France bus or public transportation into Paris and then catch a cab to wherever you're staying.

Charles de Gaulle/Roissy. If you're trying to catch a plane out of Paris, your safest bet is to take **RER B** from any Métro or RER station to **Roissy Aéroport Charles de Gaulle.** This way you won't have to worry about traffic, which can delay the buses for up to an hour. A free *navette* (shuttle bus) takes you between the airport gates and the RER station in both directions. Tickets for the 45-minute ride cost 45F, and trains leave about every 10 minutes. Trains start running at 5:30 AM toward the airport and at 6:30 AM toward town; they keep going until nearly midnight in both directions. The **ROISSYBUS,** run by the RATP, is also easy and convenient, though traffic can thwart the projected 45-minute ride time. It costs 40F, and it takes you straight from your terminal to Métro Opéra every 15 minutes from 5:45 AM to 11 PM.

Orly. Orly has two terminals: Orly-Ouest and Orly-Sud. Make sure you know which one you want. **RER C** to Orly plus a free shuttle brings you to the airport for 27F in about 30 minutes between 5:50 AM and 10:25 PM; trains in the other direction run 5:30 AM–11:30 PM. Trains in either direction leave about every 10 minutes. For 50F, you can take the **RER B** to Antony and grab the Orlyval shuttle to the airport. For 30F, the RATP-run **ORLYBUS** links the terminals with Métro Denfert-Rochereau, just south of the Quartier Latin. Look for the emblem on the side of the shuttle.

BY TRAIN Six major train stations serve Paris; all have cafés, newsstands, bureaux de change, and luggage storage. You can abandon your belongings in a locker, usually with a coded lock, for 15F–30F for 72 hours. Most train stations have tourist offices, and each is connected to the rest of Paris by the Métro system. To make a reservation from anywhere in France, call 08–36–35–35–35.

➤ **GARE D'AUSTERLITZ** • Trains from here serve **southwest France** and **Spain,** including Barcelona (10–14 hrs, 470F) and Madrid (11 hrs, 670F).

➤ **GARE DE L'EST** • This station serves **eastern France, Germany, Austria,** and **Eastern Europe,** with trains leaving daily for Frankfurt (6 hrs, 556F), Prague (16 hrs, 775F), and Vienna (13 hrs, 905F). The station is smaller than nearby Gare du Nord and its services are more limited, but there's still a tourist office and a Thomas Cook bureau de change (open daily 7 AM–6:45 PM). The neighborhood is a bit scary at night.

➤ **GARE DE LYON** • Trains from here serve the **south of France, the Alps, Switzerland,** and **Italy.** Plenty of trains run to Lyon (5 hrs, 290F), Lausanne (4 hrs, 360F), Milan (7½ hrs, 400F), and Rome (14 hrs, 640F). This is one of the bigger stations, with a full range of services, including combination luggage lockers and a bureau de change (open 7 AM–11 PM).

➤ **GARE MONTPARNASSE** • Trains travel from here to **Brittany** and **southwestern France.** Daily trains run to Bordeaux (3 hrs, 340F), Rennes (2 hrs, 260F), and Biarritz (5 hrs, 410F).

➤ **GARE DU NORD** • Trains travel from here to **northern France** (Calais and Lille), and to **Belgium,** the **Netherlands,** and points in **Scandinavia.** Regular trains run to Amsterdam (6 hrs, 390F), Copenhagen (16 hrs, 1010F), and London (*see* Coming and Going, By Eurotunnel, in Chapter 1). Showers cost 20F; soap and towels are extra. The neighborhood gets sketchy at night.

➤ **GARE ST-LAZARE** • This station serves **Normandy** and some destinations in **northern France.** International destinations include Amsterdam (6 hrs, 390F). This is the only major station without a tourist office.

BY BUS Eurolines, Paris's lone bus company, offers international service only. If you take a bus into Paris, it will most likely drop you off at the Eurolines office close to Métro Gallieni. Some of its most popular routes are to London (9 hrs, 340F), Barcelona (15 hrs, 480F), and Berlin (12 hrs, 410F). The company's international buses also arrive and depart from Avignon, Bordeaux, Lille, Lyon, Toulouse, and Tours. Unfortunately, Eurail passes don't get you any discount. *28 av. du Général-de-Gaulle, Bagnolet, tel. 01–49–72–51–51. Métro: Gallieni. Other location: 55 rue St-Jacques, 5e, tel. 01–43–54–11–99. Métro: Cluny–La Sorbonne. Both open daily 9–6.*

GETTING AROUND

If you don't get anything else straight, for God's sake learn the difference between the **Rive Gauche** (Left Bank) and the **Rive Droite** (Right Bank) before you step off that plane. The simplest directions will refer to these two sides of the Seine River, and if you have to ask which is which, you're likely to be looked at scoldingly. In the most stereotypical terms, the Rive Gauche is the artistic area; the Sorbonne and the Quartier Latin are here, along with many other bustling neighborhoods full of young people. The Rive Droite, on the other hand, is traditionally more elegant and commercial, though its less central areas are actually much cooler than the Left Bank. It's home to ritzy shopping districts and most of the big-name sights like the Louvre and the Arc de Triomphe. Between the two banks you have the Ile de la Cité, where you'll find the Cathédrale de Notre-Dame, and the smaller Ile St-Louis.

Once you have the Left and Right Banks figured out, move on to the **arrondissements,** or districts, numbered 1 through 20. (For all addresses in this book, the arrondissement number is given, since it's the most common way to describe a location.) Arrondissements one through eight are the most central and contain most of the big tourist attractions, while the ninth through 20th gradually spiral out toward the outskirts of the city.

More than two million people somehow manage to cram themselves into the apartments, cafés, restaurants, bars, and streets of Paris. The long-running joke is that the streets—narrow, winding, labyrinthine, and vertiginous—were paved according to the paths the cows wandered in more pastoral times. You *will* get lost—hell, most of the natives do, too. But that's part of the fun.

To figure out the zip code of any point in Paris, just tack the arrondissement number onto the digits 750. For example, for the fifth arrondissement, 5e, the five-digit zip code would be 75005—turning 5 into 05.

When you've had enough walking and you just want to *get there,* the city has an excellent public transportation system consisting of the Métro (the subway system) and the municipal bus system, both operated by **RATP.** If you plan to stay in Paris for only a short time, stick to the Métro; it's easier to use than the buses. To avoid getting lost on a regular basis, buy a *Plan de Paris par Arrondissement,* a booklet of detailed maps showing all Métro stops and sights, as soon as you arrive. An index at the front alphabetically lists all streets and their arrondissement. It costs 35F–60F and is available at most bookstores. You can also get less useful but free maps from the tourist offices (*see* Visitor Information, *above*). For info on all public transport, call 08–36–68–77–14 between 6 AM and 9 PM.

BY METRO AND RER   Except for the fact that it closes soon after midnight, the Métro is the epitome of convenient public transportation. Thirteen Métro lines and five main RER lines crisscross Paris and the suburbs, and you will almost never be more than a 10-minute walk from the nearest Métro stop. Any station or tourist office can give you a free map of the whole system, or you can use the handy color map at the front of this book. Métro lines are marked in the station both by line number and by the names of the stops at the end of each line. Find the number of the line you want to take and the name of the terminus toward which you will be traveling, and follow the signs.

To transfer to a different line, look for orange signs saying CORRRESPONDENCE and for the new line number and terminus you need. The blue-and-white signs that say SORTIE (exit) will lead you back above ground. You can identify Métro stations by the illuminated yellow M signs, by the round red-and-white METRO signs, or by the old, green, art nouveau arches bearing the full name, METROPOLITAIN. The Métro tends to be pretty safe at night, but bringing a companion is always a good idea.

The first Métro of the day heads out at 5:30 AM, the last at 12:30 AM. Often the directional signs on the *quais* (platforms) indicate the times at which the first and last trains pass that station. Individual tickets cost 7F, but it's much more economical to buy a *carnet* (book of 10) for 45F. You can use one ticket each time you go underground for as many transfers as you like. For extended stays consider getting a **Carte Orange,** for which you need a picture of yourself. (Large Métro stations usually have photo booths that cost 20F, and many film stores offer passport photos.) You can fill the card with a *coupon semaine* (weekly pass; 67F, valid Mon.–Sun.) or *coupon mensuel* (monthly pass; 230F, valid from the first day of the month). You can buy these at any *tabac* (tobacco shop) with the abbreviation "RATP" on the window. Whatever you use, hang on to your ticket until you exit the Métro in case some uniformed French dude wants to see it, a particular danger toward the end of the month. Young people who hop the barriers get a rough word from the attendant—or a fine of up to 250F.

Several Métro stations also act as **RER** stations. The RER is a high-speed rail system that extends into the Parisian suburbs and is a fast way to travel between major points in the city. The five principal RER lines are also marked on the Métro maps. You can use normal Métro tickets on them within Zones 1 and 2, which will get you pretty much anywhere in Paris. To venture farther into Zones 3–5—to Versailles, for example, or to the airports—you need to buy a separate, more expensive ticket.

Most of Paris's Métro lines (like the bus system) are unfortunately inaccessible to travelers with disabilities, but the RER is slightly more accessible. For more details, ask the **Régie Autonome**

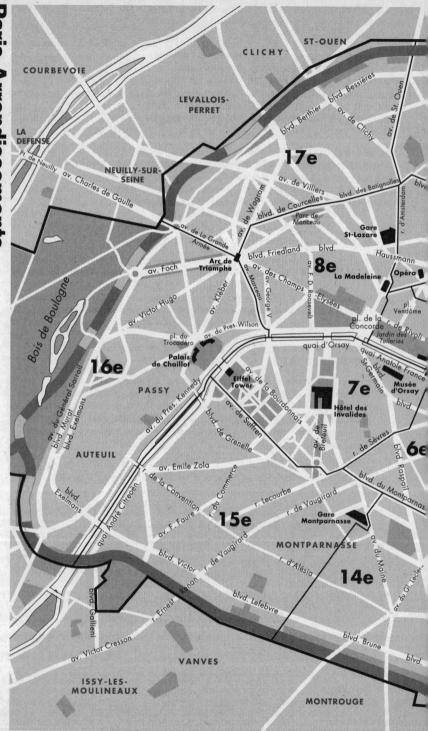

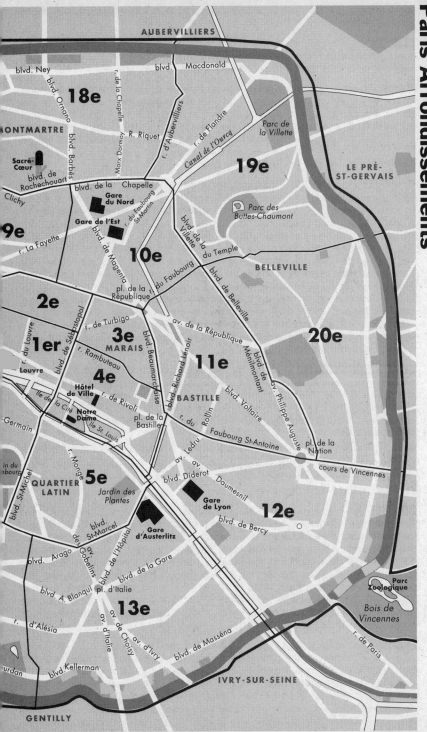

AUBERVILLIERS

blvd. Ney

blvd. Ornano

18e

r. de la Chapelle

blvd. Macdonald

R. Riquet

r. d'Aubervilliers

r. de Flandre

Canal de l'Ourcq

Parc de la Villette

19e

LE PRÉ-ST-GERVAIS

MONTMARTRE

Sacré-Cœur

blvd. Barbès

blvd. de Rochechouart

Clichy

blvd. de la Chapelle

Gare du Nord

Gare de l'Est

r. du Faubourg St-Martin

Parc des Buttes-Chaumont

9e

r. La Fayette

blvd. de Magenta

10e

du Temple

blvd. de la Villette

BELLEVILLE

2e

r. du Louvre

blvd. de Sébastopol

pl. de la République

r. de Turbigo

r. du Faubourg

blvd. de Belleville

av. de la République

20e

1er

3e

MARAIS

r. Rambuteau

blvd. Beaumarchais

blvd. Richard Lenoir

11e

blvd. de Ménilmontant

av. Philippe Auguste

Louvre

4e

Hôtel de Ville

r. de Rivoli

BASTILLE

blvd. Voltaire

Île de la Cité

Notre Dame

Île St-Louis

pl. de la Bastille

r. du Rollin

Faubourg St-Antoine

pl. de la Nation

-Germain

r. Monge

av. Ledru

blvd. Diderot

Daumesnil

cours de Vincennes

in du bourg

blvd. St-Michel

QUARTIER LATIN

5e

Jardin des Plantes

Gare de Lyon

12e

blvd. St-Marcel

Gare d'Austerlitz

blvd. de Bercy

blvd. Arago

av. des Gobelins

blvd. de l'Hôpital

blvd. de la Gare

Parc Zoologique

blvd. A. Blanqui

pl. d'Italie

Bois de Vincennes

r. d'Alésia

13e

av. de Choisy

av. d'Italie

av. d'Ivry

blvd. de Masséna

r. de Paris

urdan

blvd. Kellerman

IVRY-SUR-SEINE

GENTILLY

des **Transports Parisiens** (**RATP**) (pl. de la Madeleine, 8e, tel. 01–40–46–42–17) for its brochure on accessibility.

BY BUS The buses are safe, and they offer the distinct advantage of letting you see where you're going, how you're getting there, and anything interesting along the way. During rush hour they offer the distinct disadvantage of getting you there verrry, verrry slowly.

Métro tickets are accepted on the buses. Theoretically you need one to three tickets, depending on how far you're going, but it is highly unlikely anyone's going to check up on how many you use. In fact, even a *used* Métro ticket will fly on most buses if you're subtle and don't mind a slight risk factor. If you're caught, though, you'll have to pay an 80F fine. Stamp your ticket in the machine at the front of the bus. If you have a Carte Orange, though, don't *ever* stamp it, or it will become invalid—just flash it to the driver.

The Noctambus is a good way to meet drunk people of all nationalities and possibly learn some dirty songs in French.

There are maps of the bus system at most bus stops; all 63 bus lines run Monday through Saturday from 6:30 AM to 8:30 PM, with limited service until 12:30 AM and all day on Sunday. A handy little service, the **Noctambus,** runs 10 lines every hour on the half hour between 1:30 AM and 5:30 AM; all lines start at Métro Châtelet, leaving from just in front of the Hôtel de Ville. Stops served by the Noctambus have a yellow-and-black owl symbol on them. Technically, a single ride gobbles up four tickets, though rarely does anyone pay all four; a monthly or weekly Carte Orange works on Noctambuses, too. For a map of the night-bus routes, ask for a "Grand Plan de Paris" at any Métro station; the Noctambus lines are drawn in the corner. April 15 through September, on Sundays and holidays from noon until 9, the RATP runs a bus line called the **Balabus,** which hits all major sights in the city and takes about an hour one-way. Buses start at the La Défense or Gare de Lyon Métro stations and stop at all bus stops with the sign BB-BALABUS. The full ride costs three normal tickets, though again you can probably get away with stamping just one.

BY BIKE AND SCOOTER If you feel brave enough to face Parisian drivers and bumpy cobblestones, you can zip around on a scooter or a bike. A good place to pick up a scooter is **Mondial Scooter** (14 rue St-Maur, 11e, tel. 01–43–48–65–80) or **Dynamic Sport** (149 rue Montmartre, 2e, tel. 01–42–33–61–82), if you're willing to part with 150F–300F per day. To buy a used moped or motorcycle, check the listings in *Argus,* a weekly publication available at most newsstands.

Paris-Vélo rents bikes for 90F per day, 140F for 24 hours, 160F for two days and one night, and 500F per week. You have to provide a hefty 2,000F deposit, but they accept MasterCard and Visa. *2 rue du Fer-à-Moulin, 5e, tel. 01–43–37–59–22. Métro: Censier-Daubenton. Open Mon.–Sat. 10–12:30 and 2–7.*

BY TAXI Getting a taxi in Paris can be frustrating, especially in summer. During peak times (7–10 AM and 4–7 PM), allow yourself a couple of hours to secure one—only taxis with lit signs are available, and these are few and far between. Your chances of picking one up are best at major hotels. In the better-traveled parts of the city, people line up at makeshift taxi stations; try to find one of these, or call individual taxi companies. Rates are approximately 8F per kilometer; they may go up a bit after dark, but not more than 50 centimes or so per kilometer. Two good companies are **Taxis Radio 7000** (tel. 01–42–70–00–42) and **Taxis Bleus** (tel. 01–49–36–10–10). Your taxi driver may be able to sputter an English word or two, but don't expect him or her to understand complicated directions; a map, finger, and half-coherent verb phrase ought to do the trick.

BY BOAT During the summer, hordes of **bateaux mouches** (tel. 01–40–76–99–99) creep up and down the river, offering commentary in five languages and shining floodlights on the buildings at night. The lights show off the buildings (and the flies that give these "fly boats" their name) to their best advantage, but they make people living along the river mad as hell. Dress warmly enough to ride on the upper deck, and you might avoid the crush below. Board the boat for a 40F, 1¼-hour tour at the Pont de l'Alma. From April to September, a less touristy alternative is **Bateaux Parisiens** (tel. 01–44–11–33–55), a small boat-bus that runs between

Pont de la Bourdonnais at the Eiffel Tower and the Hôtel de Ville. There are five stations along the way, and you'll pay 20F for the journey from Hôtel de Ville to the Eiffel Tower; 60F gets you a day pass to the whole line. The boats begin running daily at 10 AM and leave about every 30 minutes until 9 PM.

Where to Sleep

Unless you have well-placed friends, Paris is not the cheapest place to spend a night. Hotels start at 100F, and that's for a dingy fleabag room with a cigarette-burned bedspread. That said, checking into a 150F hotel usually means you're laying your body on something clean, dealing with someone nice, and leaving your bags somewhere safe. Neighborhood has a lot to do with how far that "usually" goes. Monument-seekers might be happiest in the pricier neighborhoods around the **Louvre** and **Opéra**. If nightlife is your raison d'être, you'll probably want to crash in **Les Halles**, the **Marais**, or the **Bastille**. Paris's cheapest hotels are a bit farther from the center in **Belleville, Montmartre,** and **Montparnasse.**

In summer, reserve as far in advance as possible. Reservations usually require a credit-card number or a deposit for the first night. Even hostels book up quickly in summer—check in as early in the morning as possible. The AJF (see Visitor Information, above) specializes in student travel and can find you a cheap bed in a hostel for a 10F fee, but don't expect them to work miracles in high season. The tourist offices can find you something at the last minute, but they don't exactly specialize in cheap rooms.

BASTILLE Spreading over the 11th and 12th arrondissements, the Bastille is all about cool cafés, cheap restaurants, and more bars than you could visit in a lifetime. Proximity to the Gare de Lyon is an added bonus, and so is the fact that most of the hotels listed below will have space long after cheap sleeps in the Quartier Latin and the Marais are gone.

Rues with a View: Scenic Bus Rides in Paris

There are several bus lines that you can ride for a good, cheap tour of Paris, sans irritating commentary. Some of these lines are traveled by buses with small balconies at the rear, though the proximity to gusts of carbon monoxide is less than pleasant.

- *No. 29: The interesting section of the 29 stretches from Gare St-Lazare, past Opéra Garnier and the Pompidou, and through the heart of the Marais, crossing the place des Vosges before ending up at the Bastille. This is one of the few lines that run primarily through the small streets of a neighborhood, and it has an open back.*

- *No. 69: Get on at the Champ de Mars (the park right by the Eiffel Tower) and ride through parts of the Quartier Latin, across the bridge to the Right Bank near the Louvre, by the Hôtel de Ville (City Hall), and out to the Bastille area.*

- *No. 72: River lovers will appreciate this line. It follows the Seine from the Hôtel de Ville east past the city limits, hitting the Louvre, the Trocadéro, and most of the big-name Right Bank sights. You also get good views of the Left Bank, including the Eiffel Tower.*

- *Montmartrobus: If you want to see all of Montmartre without facing the hills "à pied" (by foot), pick up this bus at Pigalle for a winding tour of the area, including a pass under the Sacré Coeur. No special ticket is needed.*

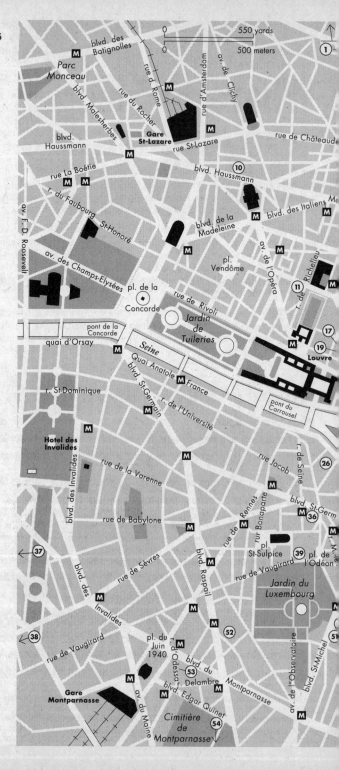

Hôtel Henri IV, **25**
Hôtel Jean Bart, **52**
Hôtel La Fayette, **7**
Hôtel
La Marmotte, **12**
Hôtel le
Central, **47**
Hôtel Métropole La
Fayette, **8**
Hôtel Marignan, **42**
Hôtel Nouvel
France, **31**
Hôtel Practic, **27**
Hôtel Richelieu
Mazarin, **11**
Hôtel Rivoli, **23**
Hôtel Stella, **40**
Hôtel Surcouf, **4**
Idéal Hôtel, **1**
Maison des Clubs
UNESCO de
Paris, **56**
Maison des
Etudiants, **19**
Maison
Internationale des
Jeunes, **34**
Modern's Hôtel, **45**
Nadaud Hôtel, **14**
Pax Hôtel, **29**
Sainte Bastille
Opéra, **33**
Sully Hôtel, **28**
Three Ducks
Hostel, **37**
Université de Paris
Foyer International
des Etudiantes, **51**
Young and Happy
Youth Hostel, **58**

➤ **UNDER 175F** • **Hôtel Nouvel France.** This place is pretty squalid, but the price and location (amidst the Bastille's bars and galleries) can't be beat. Singles start at 120F, doubles at 150F (180F with shower). *31 rue Keller, 11e, tel. 01–47–00–40–74. Métro: Bastille or Voltaire. From Bastille, walk down rue de la Roquette, turn right on rue Keller. 47 rooms, 5 with bath. Showers free.*

Modern's Hôtel. Clean, quiet rooms are only steps away from the Gare de Lyon. Singles are 140F, doubles 150F (210F with shower). *11 rue d'Austerlitz, near rue de Lyon, 12e, tel. 01–43–43–41–17. Métro: Gare de Lyon. 30 rooms, 14 with bath. Breakfast 20F, extra bed 40F, showers 15F.*

Sainte Bastille Opéra. This modest hotel is in the heart of the Bastille, only 15 seconds from the Opéra Bastille and the lively rue de Lappe. Singles start at 120F, doubles at 160F. *6 rue de la Roquette, 11e, tel. 01–43–55–16–06. Métro: Bastille. 19 rooms, none with bath. Showers free.*

➤ **UNDER 200F** • **Hôtel de l'Europe.** This professional outfit offers big, clean, comfy rooms—it's worth calling ahead. Singles and doubles are 185F, with shower 210F–230F. *74 rue Sedaine, 11e, tel. 01–47–00–54–38, fax 01–47–00–75–31. Métro: Voltaire. 26 rooms, 15 with bath. Breakfast 20F, extra bed 60F, showers 10F.*

➤ **UNDER 225F** • **Hôtel Baudin.** Big, colorful, homey rooms and a good location make this a great place to stay. Singles are 120F–210F, doubles 200F. Be sure to reserve in advance. *113 av. Ledru-Rollin, 11e, tel. 01–47–00–18–91. Métro: Ledru Rollin. 19 rooms, 7 with shower. Breakfast 25F, showers 20F. Reservations advised. AE, V.*

Pax Hôtel. The Pax's clean rooms and fabulous location make up for the chilly reception toward the backpacking set. Singles and doubles without shower are 220F–230F, or live it up with full bath, phone, and color TV for 300F–400F. *12 rue de Charonne, 11e, tel. 01–47–00–40–98. Métro: Ledru Rollin. 47 rooms, 40 with bath. Breakfast 30F. MC, V.*

BELLEVILLE Belleville, an immigrant neighborhood in the northern part of the 20th arrondissement above Père-Lachaise, is not exactly a lodging mecca. Look around **place Gambetta** for hotels, but be careful wandering alone at night.

➤ **UNDER 125F** • **Hôtel de Bordeaux.** This large hotel sits near a busy intersection close to heaps of cheap restaurants. The dark rooms are a little grim, but they're fairly clean, safe, and cheap: Singles are 100F–120F, doubles 120F–160F (200F with bath). *3 rue Lémon, at blvd. de Belleville, 20e, tel. 01–40–33–98–15. Métro: Belleville. 66 rooms, 34 with bath.*

➤ **UNDER 175F** • **Hôtel du Chemin de Fer.** Though the cheaper rooms are dingy, you'll be in a relatively calm and safe section of Belleville and just 60 seconds from Père-Lachaise. Singles or doubles are 170F (200F and up with shower). *233 rue des Pyrénées, 20e, tel. 01–43–58–55–18. Métro: Gambetta. 33 rooms, 26 with shower. Showers 18F. AE, MC, V.*

➤ **UNDER 200F** • **Nadaud Hôtel.** The rooms, some with gorgeous views of Paris, are more than worth the price—195F and up (275F with shower). Reserve a week in advance. *8 rue de la Bidassoa, near av. Gambetta, 20e, tel. 01–46–36–87–79, fax 01–46–36–05–41. Métro: Gambetta. 22 rooms, 13 with shower. Breakfast 27F, showers 20F. MC, V.*

GARE DE L'EST AND GARE DU NORD This is a great area if you arrive late, don't have a reservation, and are too tired to drag your belongings any farther. But stay away if you value peace and quiet (traffic roars all night long) or your wallet—foreign visitors have reported thefts here. If the hotels below are booked, walk straight for one block from either station to **boulevard de Magenta** and its budget hotels.

➤ **UNDER 150F** • **Hôtel La Fayette.** The rooms here are clean, modest, and simple. Singles are 110F, doubles 135F–155F. The lone room with a shower costs 226F. *198 rue La Fayette, 10e, tel. 01–40–35–76–07, fax 01–42–09–69–05. Métro: Louis Blanc. 21 rooms. Breakfast 20F, showers 20F. AE, MC, V.*